# NEW APPROACHES TO CREATING A CULTURE OF INNOVATION

T0285260

# THE NEW BUSINESS CULTURE SERIES

# NEW APPROACHES TO CREATING A CULTURE OF INNOVATION

BY

## FONS TROMPENAARS

*Trompenaars Hampden-Turner Consulting,
The Netherlands*

*and*

## PETER WOOLLIAMS

*Anglia Ruskin, Cambridge, UK*

United Kingdom – North America – Japan – India
Malaysia – China

Emerald Publishing Limited
Emerald Publishing, Floor 5, Northspring, 21-23 Wellington Street, Leeds LS1 4DL.

First edition 2025

Copyright © 2025 Fons Trompenaars and Peter Woolliams.
Published under exclusive licence by Emerald Publishing Limited.

**Reprints and permissions service**
Contact: www.copyright.com

No part of this book may be reproduced, stored in a retrieval system, transmitted in any
form or by any means electronic, mechanical, photocopying, recording or otherwise
without either the prior written permission of the publisher or a licence permitting
restricted copying issued in the UK by The Copyright Licensing Agency and in the USA
by The Copyright Clearance Center. No responsibility is accepted for the accuracy
of information contained in the text, illustrations or advertisements. The opinions
expressed in these chapters are not necessarily those of the Author or the publisher.

**British Library Cataloguing in Publication Data**
A catalogue record for this book is available from the British Library

ISBN: 978-1-83608-457-0 (Print)
ISBN: 978-1-83608-454-9 (Online)
ISBN: 978-1-83608-456-3 (Epub)

INVESTOR IN PEOPLE

# CONTENTS

# LIST OF FIGURES AND TABLES

## FIGURES

## TABLES

# ABOUT THE AUTHORS

**Fons Trompenaars**, PhD, is Director of Trompenaars Hampden-Turner (THT) Consulting, an innovative centre of excellence on intercultural management. He is the world's foremost authority on cross-cultural management and is author of many books and related articles. He is CEO of THT Consulting and Culture Factory and Visiting Professor at The Free University of Amsterdam.

**Peter Woolliams**, PhD, is Professor Emeritus of International Management at Anglia Ruskin, Cambridge, UK and is a partner in Trompenaars Hampden-Turner (THT) Consulting and its technical subsidiary Culture Factory. He has collaborated and published jointly with Fons over some 25 years. He has worked with Fons to develop a whole series of diagnostic apps and profiling tools and cultural databases which has led to the creation of the intellectual property of THT Consulting.

# RATIONALE FOR THE SERIES

The business environment continues to change ever more rapidly. Established practice is constantly challenged in our post-COVID-19, climate changing, and technology-driven world leading to the further proliferation of digitalisation, new flexible ways and places of working, leadership styles, diversity, etc. All areas of business and management are finding that traditional frameworks for organisation design, marketing, HR, and other functional disciplines no longer provide models for best practice. Not only driven by such changes in the external environment but together with the differing value systems of younger generations there is an urgent need to provide new frames of reference that can help formulate new business strategies while synergising with the career aspirations of the labour market.

The New Business Culture is a series of micro-books with each addressing an area of business and management that seeks to demonstrate how and where established traditional models and frameworks are no longer providing optimum frameworks for the purpose that informs the range of subject areas discussed. The authors offer new approaches that transcend convention.

In this series of volumes, each distils the essential elements of a key topic and retains focus and purpose and seeks to offer new approaches to overcome the limitations of existing practice.

The content and new concepts therein originate from the synergy between the authors own fundamental research (including supervision of PhD students) triangulated with evidence and application from their extensive client base in their consulting practice (THT Consulting, Amsterdam).

Purchase of each volume in the series includes exclusive access to a corresponding companion App. Each App enables readers to explore the application of specific concepts in further detail for individual volumes and what it means for them and/or their organisation.

# 1

# INTRODUCTION

In a world where businesses are increasingly dominated by a few powerful players and ideas can be easily duplicated at a lower cost, it's crucial for the survival of organisations (of all sizes) to constantly come up with new and creative solutions to differentiate themselves from others in their increasingly oligopolistic market. As early as IBM's study[1] of Global CEOs (2006) reported that leaders across industries and regions were seeking to shift their focus from cost-cutting to sustained growth through innovation. The study found that CEOs saw innovation as the key to achieving organic growth and building brand value. Rather than just focussing on inventing new products or processes, CEOs were increasingly placing emphasis on differentiating their business models through innovative approaches.

The business, economic, and academic press has continued to report the need for a priori innovation and that innovation has to become central to organisation life, taking on new shapes and processes that go beyond traditional concepts.

Some companies such as Apple were of course born innovative but for the majority, whence initial success comes from a single good idea, being in the right place at the right time, a shift from their initial beneficial intransigence to constant change is difficult.

## 1.1. LIMITATIONS OF EXTANT KNOWLEDGE

In spite of much published research on creativity per se, there is still an absence of an organised body of knowledge to inform professional practice as to how

---

1 Expanding the Innovation Horizon, the Global CEO study 2006, IBM Global Services, New York, USA, 2006.

organisations can overcome the inertia in transitioning from their current ways of working. We can identify several reasons as detailed in the sections.

## 1.2. THE COMMODIFICATION OF EDUCATION

Experts like Glickman,[2] Mintzberg,[3] and Russell Ackoff[4] have highlighted that schools tend to prioritise instilling conservative thinking in children that aligns with their parents' beliefs. Teachers may unknowingly prioritise finding the 'correct' solution the teacher knows rather than encouraging students to find alternative solutions. This narrow approach limits the exploration of new ideas. So creativity can be described as the process of breaking the assumptions one has accumulated unconsciously through one's collective programming through education, upbringing, and/or culture. The teaching of creativity has a lot to do with revealing the common property of solutions, and breaking the assumption that the solver imposed on the problem.

Lots of exercises were designed to install a sense of creativity (although usually with little supporting evidence to their value).

How many golf balls would it take to fill a jumbo jet? Estimate how many windows there are in Fifth Avenue, New York (or Oxford Street, London), or how many ways can you use a paper clip?

Anyone who has studied for an MBA knows this puzzle. Can you connect nine dots with four straight lines without lifting the pen from the paper?

### VIGNETTE: THAT NINE DOTS PUZZLE

Many MBA students believe that thinking outside the box is the key to finding solutions. One student, Ackoff's daughter, asked her father for advice and he suggested folding the paper in a way that the dots would overlap, using only one line instead of four. When the teacher asked the class for solutions, only five people raised their hands. Four of them gave

---

2   Carl D. Glickman (Editor), Letters to the next president: What we can do about the real crisis in public education, Teachers College Press (February 2004).

3   Henry Mintzberg, Managers not MBAs: A hard look at the soft practice of managing and management development, Berrett-Koehler Publishers (1 January 2004).

4   Russell L. Ackoff, The art of problem solving, p. 5, Wiley Inter-Science, 1978.

the common solution, while Ackoff's daughter angry and refused, insisting that the only acceptable solution was the one she knew.

Ackoff believed that this is how creativity is suppressed in some cases. The objective of an assignment should not be to find a specific solution, but rather to encourage students to think beyond the obvious options and break away from assumptions learned through education, upbringing, and culture. To teach creativity, it is important to reveal the common properties of solutions and challenge assumptions.

As Ackoff observes:

'A puzzle is a problem that one cannot solve because of a self-imposed constraint. Creativity is shackled by self-imposed constraints. Therefore, the key to freeing it lies in developing an ability to identify such constraints and deliberately removing them'.

Our traditional Western education might not help us to remove self-imposed constraints. On the contrary, it might even add some more. And very often, this doesn't stop simply in the academic educational environment: in business too, we have to focus on what MBA education and in-service training have done to our creativity.

'Conventional MBA programs train the wrong people in the wrong ways with the wrong consequences', states Mintzberg, who proposes drastic changes in our traditional form of management education. He discovered a profound 'disconnect between the practice of management ... and what went on in classrooms'. Using words like 'arrogance', 'mindless' and 'exploitation', Mintzberg criticises MBAs and their degrees, pointing out flaws in both. He believes that his own model, based on real-world experience, is more relevant and valuable to students, companies, and the business world. Mintzberg argues that good management, not business schools, drives innovative economies. He claims that the top MBAs are often products of an unrealistic graduate programme, which has negative effects beyond the classroom.

According to Mintzberg, there are three major obstacles to the creative mind of an MBA student:

- First, the assumption that there is only one best approach to solving business problems.

- Second, the assumption that the business world is linear and excludes alternatives.

- Finally, education often focusses on controlling the business environment and avoiding mistakes, which stifles creativity.

So why did we get to this state of affairs?

Let's remember that Universities created MBA's and other 'conversion' Master's as a new cash cow. Let's consider ...

Historically, students first studied for their undergraduate Bachelor's degree. Content was learning established extant knowledge, from lectures and textbooks written by their tutors. It was a catching up exercise, learning to know the basics of their topic, and remained more or less static over time. On graduation, they could opt to proceed to a Master's degree IN THE SAME SUBJECT DOMAIN. The content was evolving knowledge and thus based on both the new knowledge being created by their department's researchers and current credible research publications and current cases from practice. And was continually updated year on year. It was described as post-graduate and never used the term 'advanced' – as in advanced degree level. Selected top gun students may be given the chance to research for a PhD where the focus was on creating new knowledge through research under the guidance of their professors.

Particularly around the 1960s, industry lobbied politicians to complain that graduates holding a Bachelor's degree didn't know anything about the real world and needed further education to charge them with some real-world knowledge.

And so was born the 'conversion masters'. An engineering student with a Bachelor's degree in Engineering could spend another year studying for a Master's degree in Business or even part-time over a longer time scale. But these were post-graduate in time rather than post-graduate in level. Universities rubbed their hands with their new income-generating model. All the teaching staff had to do was spell out the same content they were normally teaching on the Bachelor's degree in business studies (much of it out of date and irrelevant). Better universities rebranded the Master's degree in Business as the American sounding Master's in Business Administration. In this way, it was claimed a technically competent (e.g. engineer) could be 'converted' to being employable in the world of business.

Years later, some business education has improved, but the total system has still not changed to recognise the need to support creativity with emphasis still on out-of-date content.

We have our own evidence in making the above statement. As indicated earlier, the content and new concepts in this and other books in this series originate from the synergy between the authors own fundamental research (including supervision of PhD students) triangulated with evidence and application from their extensive client base in their consulting practice (THT Consulting, Amsterdam). We continue to find many business studies students still being taught[5] out-of-date

---

5  We must reserve some sympathy for academic staff who have not always received the level of support from governments through their university for ongoing in-service development due to pressures on higher-education funding.

conceptual models for leadership, culture, research methods, etc. – not in the best interests of students or indeed the future labour market for their services. Obviously acceptable if clear they are earlier models and are followed by current practice and current theory.

## 1.3. LACK OF JOINED UP THINKING

Currently, we are witnessing two trends in the business world: increasing standardisation and ever-growing diversity. The key to new innovation lies in connecting these two trends. Effective leadership involves bringing together both shared and differing aspects. Unfortunately, we are lacking this type of leadership in today's world.

The reductionist approach to science has led to highly segmented domains of creativity, invention, and business development. There is no generalisable theory that can help leaders, HR professionals, or team leaders in today's world.

The conventional investigative approaches have limitations, particularly in terms of research design. These limitations can affect the development of new, generalisable theories that can apply across various subject domains. According to conventional wisdom, researchers must choose between positivist and inter-pretivist inquiry, whether qualitative or quantitative. Mixed methodologies are seen as a compromise solution, which can limit our thinking and modelling of reality. This issue is explored further in the body of this book.

To innovate, we not only need to develop new theories, but also a new paradigm of inquiry and an associated methodological approach to research and describe it.

Our own research suggests that creativity and innovation arise from reconciling standardisation with diversity through leadership. There are encouraging developments in this regard, given the growing internationalisation of business and the increasing number of inter-organisational activities that energise creativity. Even American culture has realised that imposing a standardised logic on the world (especially their own) doesn't work well, neither in business nor in politics. While the world may become flat in some ways, as Friedman[6] suggests, it is also spiky, as Richard Florida[7] demonstrates.

In order for an organisation to be innovative, it must nurture creativity at three key levels: the individual, the team and the organisation as a whole. While having creative individuals is essential, simply putting them together may not result in a creative team. It is important to have people with complementary

---

6 Thomas L. Friedman, The world is flat: A brief history of the twenty-first century, Farrar, Straus and Giroux; expanded and updated edition, 18 April 2006.

7 Richard Florida, The world is spiky, The Atlantic Monthly, October 2005.

skills working together to foster inventiveness. We've all witnessed organisations with excellent research and development (R&D) and marketing teams that cannot effectively work together and end up being dysfunctional. The R&D teams at a major pharmaceutical company we helped complained bitterly that their marketing department paid insufficient attempt to sell their new ideas in the market. Whereas, the marketing department claimed bitterly, 'why can't our R&D people come up with what our customers want?'

To create an innovative organisation, it is crucial to establish a pattern of interactions where individuals and teams work effectively together towards a common goal.

## 1.4. RESEARCH QUESTIONS

To address the lack of a clear theory base to guide professional practice and the limitations of existing knowledge in various disciplines, we began our interest in innovation based on the following (albeit at the meta level initially) research questions:

- What are the limitations of traditional paradigms of inquiry (such as positivism and interpretivism) in researching creativity and innovation?

- What new insights can be gained by integrating theories of creativity and innovation through an innovative research approach based on non-bipolar 'through-through' thinking?

- Can existing models be applied, extended, and improved to make them transferable across cultures?

- Can an integrative approach be developed that is generalisable and can inform professional practice?

Our new approach seeks to explore the limitations of models based on classical paradigms of inquiry and associated methodologies. To achieve this, we have avoided the traditional choices between positivist or interpretative methodologies, deductive or inductive approaches, and quantitative or qualitative methods. Instead, we have adopted a 'dilemmaism' approach, which involves always considering the opposite of any perspective and exploring how they can be reconciled. By framing questions and challenges as dilemmas, we can map and extend them, ultimately leading to solutions.

Our research gathered primary data originates through face-to-face interviews with business leaders and innovators from various industries and functional disciplines. Additionally, we utilised web technology to capture responses from 150,000 plus respondents worldwide, resulting in nearly 60,000 dilemmas, value, and cultural orientations.

We subjected the data to rigorous mining and analysis, including classical factor and linguistic analysis of textual responses. Through triangulation of interviews, soft data, and hard data, we found high reliability and validity in our findings.

## 1.5. OVERVIEW OF OUR NEW APPROACH

Our approach offers a new conceptual model that expands on established theories of creativity and innovation. Our goal is to provide a framework for developing more creative individuals and cultivating a culture of innovation within organisations continually reminding ourselves that in today's business landscape, where old ideas can be easily replicated, the ability to constantly generate creative solutions is the key to survival.

The core philosophy of this framework centres around developing individuals first, then teams, and ultimately the entire organisation in order to sustain long-term growth and success. This requires a shift away from simplistic linear thinking and binary decision-making, which is often influenced by cultural biases and education.

Our research shows that creativity requires a nuanced approach that combines opposing options to create something new. This new construct for 'making connections' is the foundation of the proposed new approaches we offer which is also a new conceptual model as a basis for new theory.

This book highlights the importance of leaders and managers creating a supportive environment that fosters creativity and innovation in order to achieve business objectives and solve issues. One of our colleagues, Charles Hampden-Turner, once said that innovation involves combining values that are not easily joined, which makes them scarce and profitable. Apple has become an icon of innovation by combining functionality with aesthetics. They believe that everything that is beautiful should also have a function. For example, the glass plate without a frame is not only visually appealing but also practical as it prevents the user from breaking their nails when swiping it. This approach is similar to that of Formula One, where seemingly contradicting values like speed and safety are combined to enhance the overall performance of the car. Engineers in Formula One ask themselves how they can use speed to improve the safety of the car, and aerodynamics is the answer. The faster the car goes, the more downforce it produces, making it safer and faster at the same time.

This book is aimed at helping business leaders and managers understand the impact their behaviours have on their employees and how to align the needs of the organisation with those of their employees. It is also for individuals and students in the field of business and management who want to learn about the importance of soft skills and organisational behaviour.

Creating a culture for innovation is a multifaceted process that requires a combination of psychological safety, empowering and inclusive leadership, continuous learning, collaboration, risk tolerance, and innovation-focussed rewards. By implementing these practices, organisations can enhance their innovation capabilities, fuel creativity, and remain competitive in a rapidly evolving business landscape.

We have continued to publish our findings from our earlier research[8] through to our recent enriched by the use of the internet to capture data from respondents to our diagnostic tools – both developmental testing versions as well operational versions for our consulting work. This includes peer review academic papers, working papers, practitioner articles and of course our portfolio of textbooks.

We have previously mentioned some of these ideas but with increasing data, more critical analysis, and parallel investigations by our PhD research students – and tested in 'real life' with our client organisations, we can claim significantly more reliability and validity in the content and updating we present in this book.

We have structured our discussions that follow in the form of the three perspectives of individuals, teams, and then the organisation.

---

8   Including: Trompenaars & Woolliams, Business across cultures (2008), Capstone; Trompenaars (2007), Riding the Whirlwind: Connecting people and organisations in a culture of innovation, Infinite Ideas Limited; and Hampden-Turner & Trompenaars (2000–2020), Riding the waves of culture, Nicholas Brealey Publishing.

# 2

# WHAT IS INDIVIDUAL CREATIVITY?

The development of an innovative culture often stems from individuals, such as entrepreneurs or creative geniuses. These individuals challenge established routines, make mistakes, and constantly learn from them. While some may believe that only artists or sculptors exhibit creativity, it is now a necessity for survival in the global economy. Anyone can become creative, but this goes against conventional thinking.

Researchers have attempted to define creativity by identifying the special skill or competence possessed by creative individuals and whether it is innate or teachable. However, there is a wide range of implicit theories regarding creativity that have not been explored systematically. Many people base their ideas on 'great man' theories, such as Leonardo da Vinci or Einstein, without being able to define creativity explicitly.

Explicit theories that have been generated typically focus on measuring a person's capacity or ability to create, rather than defining what creativity is. This approach evaluates the correctness of responses and measures ability or level of creativity based on fluency, flexibility, originality, and elaboration. The level approach is specific to the situation being examined and can be measured through various dimensions, such as[1] connections, perspective, curiosity, boldness, complexity, persistence, and abstraction.

Since the 1950s, more researchers have been studying how people express their creativity through different cognitive styles. This style approach aims to answer the question of *how* individuals are creative.

Extensive research has been conducted to identify highly creative individuals through the level approach. This has led to the belief that creativity is limited to a minority who possess the ability to generate creative thinking, while others

---

1   As used by CREAX NV, Belgium, in their 'Creativity' profiling tool.

lack it. However, most researchers conclude that everyone can be creative to some degree if given the opportunity (and encouragement and support).

In defining creativity, several authors[2] have included four characteristics:

1. it involves imaginative thinking or behaviour;

2. it is purposeful towards an objective;

3. it generates something original; and

4. is valuable in relation to the objective.

Other research has examined whether creativity levels can be enhanced through formal training. Torrance[3] et al. identified 384 studies on creativity training, with the majority concluding that it can be improved. Parnes[4] and Noller conducted one of the most extensive studies on the effects of creativity training.

As we discuss in some detail throughout this series, many research studies have limitations because they only use linear scales, which don't allow for other orientations. As a consequence, the starting point for their research arises from a particular perspective that accounts for different categories of definitions that have not yet been resolved into any unifying framework.

In summary, creativity has variously been described as:

An innate trait.

A soft skill.

A collection of skills that together embody creativity.

A competence (=has the knowledge to).

A competency (=exhibits creativity in his/her behaviour).

And from a more behavioural perspective as listed in Table 1.

---

2   Example Guilford, J.P., Way beyond the IQ, Buffalo, NY: Beady Limited, 1977.

3   Torrance, E. P., Torrance tests of creative thinking: Norms and technical manual, Bensenville, IL: Scholastic Testing Service, 1974; Torrance, E. P., 'Can we teach children to think creatively?', Journal of Creative Behaviour 6, pp. 236–262, 1972; and Torrance, E. P. and Presbury, J., 'Criteria of success of 242 recent experimental studies of creativity', Creative Child Quarterly 30, pp. 15–19, 1984.

4   Parnes, S. J. and Noller, R. B., 'Applied creativity: The creative studies project Part 11', Journal of Creative Behavior 6, pp. 164–186, 1972.

**Table 1. Describing Creativity.**

| Creative People Are More... | Creative People Are Less... |
| --- | --- |
| Intuitive | Sensing |
| Thinking | Feeling |
| Perceiving | Judging |
| Extrovert | Introvert |
| Tortoise brain | Hare brain |
| Lateral | Focussed |
| Risk-taking | Securing |
| Hunting | Gathering |
| Individualistic | Consensus seeking |
| Right brain | Left brain |

It's possible that there are connections between dominant behavioural orientations and an individual's creative competencies, but an important point has been overlooked. Some may argue that multiple studies have shown a correlation between certain preferences and creativity. As we discuss in detail in Section 2.5. The Adapter-Innovator, Kirton, a renowned British psychologist, developed the KAI Inventory,[5] a well-regarded tool for measuring individual problem-solving styles. His scale profiles respondents as to their orientation between a continuum from 'adapter' to 'innovator' on the basis that innovative creative people can invent but not implement ideas and need to partner with adapters with the skills of logistics to deliver.

In a study conducted by Kirton, he discovered a correlation between his KAI and the MBTI (Meyers Briggs Type Indicator).

The main links[6] between his KAI were with the MBTI's Sensing-Intuiting (S-N) and Judging-Perceiving (J-P) scales. Thinking-Feeling (T-F) and Introvert-Extrovert (I-E) were not highly correlated). Studies from other authors went further, and one[7] claimed that all four MBTI preferences correlate with creativity. Creative individuals tend to be more intuitive (N) than sensory (S), more

---

5   Kirton, M. J., Innovation requires adaptation. Journal of Applied Psychology 61, pp. 622–629, 1980.

6   Kirton, M. J., 'Adaptors and innovators: A description of a measure', Journal of Applied Psychology, 61, pp. 622–629, 1976.

7   Thorne, Avril and Harrison Gough, Portraits of type: An MBTI research compendium, Palo Alto, California: Consulting Psychologists Press Inc, 1991.

perceiving (P) than judging (J), more extroverted (E) than introverted (I), and more thinking (T) than feeling (F).

It is important to note that while there is a statistically reliable relationship between certain characteristics and preferences, reliability does not necessarily equate to validity. Our research (as discussed later) has shown that creativity is not limited to one end of a continuum, but rather, it is the interaction between opposite ends of the scale. Specifically, how the faculties of imagination, holism, emotions, and connectedness in the right brain interact with the preferences of the left brain for being realistic, analytic, and rational. Successful creative individuals integrate all of these faculties in order to generate new ideas and solutions.

Let's continue to take a closer look at some of the other commonly cited models of distinctive orientations to see what the limitation of linear scales means.

## 2.1. HARE BRAIN AND TORTOISE MIND

Guy Claxton[8] distinguishes between two modes of thinking: 'hare brain' and 'tortoise mind'. The former is characterised by fast, analytical, and language-dependent thought processes, but it may not always be the best tool for creative problem-solving. The latter, or 'tortoise mind', is slower and more meditative, and it excels in solving fuzzy and imprecise problems. Claxton calls this mode of thinking the 'undermind' and he argues that our best thinking often occurs below the level of consciousness. He believes that conscious, result-oriented problem-solving is only one aspect of intelligence, and that we can benefit from tapping into our unconscious intelligence, which approaches problems playfully and keeps us in touch with our poetic nature. Claxton draws on the works of poets, novelists, and Buddhist teachings to support his multidisciplinary approach, which emphasises the virtues of intuition and a peaceful mind. In contrast to the Western approach to intelligence, which values verbalisation and conscious attention, Claxton believes that much of our intelligence is unconscious and intuitive. This may explain why management fads often fail in the long run, as they rely too heavily on conscious problem-solving and overlook the value of unconscious intelligence.

---

8  Guy Claxton, Hare Brain, Tortoise Mind: How intelligence increases when you think less, Harper Perennial, 2000.

## 2.1.1. Collaborating Between the Hare Brain and Tortoise Mind

It may seem like creativity stems from the tortoise mind, but utilising both your hare brain WITH tortoise mind is what truly makes a difference. As yourself: where and under what circumstances did your best creative idea come to fruition?

Chances are, it didn't happen when you were solely exerting yourself or when you were completely relaxed and waiting for inspiration to strike. Rather, your greatest ideas likely arose from the tension between hard work and relaxation. Perhaps you were on vacation when suddenly new ideas came flooding in, making a difficult project much more manageable.

To summarise, Claxton characterises the hare brain as logical, fast, and machine-like in its thinking. The tortoise mind, on the other hand, is slower, less focussed, less articulate, and more playful or dreamy. Claxton suggests that these two sides of the brain need each other to generate not just ideas, but good ideas. It's important to note that the hare brain is necessary for gathering information and working hard on it before the tortoise mind can be effective and creative. The solutions come from hard work, so it's essential to utilise the hare brain first. Next, you must contemplate the situation, and finally, when you have ideas, you need to evaluate them logically and systematically (using the hare brain again). This creates a circular process that reconciles the tension between the hare brain and tortoise mind.

Many people believe that they make conscious decisions in their daily lives. However, Claxton argues that our mysterious 'undermind' plays a greater role in shaping who we are and what we do than our conscious, logical, linear mind. We typically rely on our deliberative thinking style, known as the 'd-mode', which we develop during our years of education. However, research suggests that the d-mode has little influence on most of our decision-making processes. While the d-mode may offer plausible justifications for our actions, it is not the source of those actions. The conscious mind's role is to direct our attention to a particular problem and maintain a coherent sense of self, but this occurs after our inner decision-making. People tend to be happier with their choices in the long run if they think less about them initially. In this sense, 'thinking less' may actually lead to more intelligent decisions.

To create the conditions for the tortoise mind, it's important to perceive oneself as creative. Creative individuals give themselves the freedom to create, while uncreative people do not. All it takes is setting aside time to step back and consider if there is a better way of doing something. Edward de Bono suggests taking a short break of only 30 seconds, which he calls a 'Creative Pause', as a habitual part of thinking. This requires self-discipline, but it's a small price to pay for fostering creativity.

## 2.2. MBTI REVISITED

The Myers-Briggs[9] Type Indicator (MBTI) is a widely used personality assessment tool that helps professionals' measure personality traits objectively. It is administered to over three million people annually and is often relied upon by Human Resources professionals to aid important business, career, or personal decisions.

The MBTI is based on the work of Carl Jung, who discovered that understanding the way we process information can provide insight into our actions and emotions. Jung identified two core psychological processes: perceiving (taking in information) and judging (processing information). He also identified two ways of perceiving information (sensing and intuiting) and two ways of judging information (thinking and feeling). These processes can be directed towards the external world (extraversion) or the internal world (introversion).

The MBTI is a helpful tool, but it has limitations when it comes to measuring creativity. To address this, the MBTI Creativity Index (MBTI-CI) has been developed to evaluate creativity. Creative individuals tend to score high in intuition, perception, extroversion, and thinking. Studies suggest that innovators often have an ENT combination, while senior organisation managers are often STJs. However, these differences in perspective can lead to conflicts between innovators and managers.

The MBTI is a tool for understanding personality types, but it has some flaws. Our concern is that it uses binary classifications, such as judging *or* perceiving, thinking, *or* feeling. However, Jung, the creator of the archetypes used in MBTI, believed in synthesis and warned against polarising personality traits. Instead, he suggested that we mature over time and use all of our faculties in balance.

The MBTI also has limitations in measuring the integration of contrasting personality types and the repression of 'shadow sides'. This is why we developed our own Integrated Type Indicator. We wanted to build on the strengths of the MBTI while also assessing the extent to which individuals have integrated their introverted and extroverted ideas, intuitions, feelings, and judgments. By doing

---

9   Isabel Myers, Gifts differing, Palo Alto, California: CPP Inc, 1995. And look at
    http://www.winovations.com/NFmbti.htm; Myers, Isabel Briggs, and Mary H.
    McCaulley, Manual: A guide to the development and use of the Myers-Briggs
    type indicator, Palo Alto, California: Consulting Psychologists Press Inc, 1992;
    and Gough, Harrison, 'Studies of the Myers-Briggs Type Indicator in a person-
    ality assessment research institute', paper presented at the Fourth National
    Conference on the Myers-Briggs Type Indicator, Stanford University, California,
    July 1981.

so, we hoped to unlock the key to creativity and expand one-dimensional models of leadership.

We have discussed MBTI further in other volumes in the series: New Approaches to Recruitment and Engagement and New Approaches to Flexible Working. We continue to discuss the limitations of MBTI here, not because of the failings of MBTI itself, but because it is so well known and used so widely in different contexts, many readers will already be familiar with it. It is just one example of a tool that is used extensively based on linear scales. As we try to make clear, our argument is with linear scales and not just MBTI, but MBTI is a useful example to elicit and explore these limitations.

As we discussed in these other volumes, that while the MBTI has been correlated with job categories and functions, we face new challenges when applying it in an international context. For example, a culture that prefers sensing may not be conducive to creating new products or services for someone who prefers intuiting. Our concern is that the single-axis continuum used in the MBTI and other profiling tools can be limiting when applied across national and/or organisation cultures.

In summary, while the MBTI has its flaws, we believe it is important to build on its strengths and develop new tools to assess personality integration and promote creativity in leadership.

To make the MBTI a more effective instrument for measuring creativity, we need to adjust its context. While there is some evidence that the typologies are related to creativity, the assumptions on which the instrument is based may limit its potential. We need a different approach and context to truly measure creativity beyond cultural preferences.

To achieve this, the MBTI needs to be redesigned into an Integrated Type Indicator that overcomes the limitations of its underlying models. The current models were designed to measure only within specific environments and delimitations. We need to question why these models rely on mutually exclusive values and consider a broader framework that is not limited by Western thinking's either/or mentality. Jung's original conceptual framework[10] behind the MBTI was not intended to be so limiting, and we should keep this in mind as we move forward.

The preference for using our dominant hand when writing, as discussed by professional psychologists, may not be a practical solution. Although one hand is usually dominant, both can be used.

While MBTI users discuss combining preferences in teams and organisations, this approach isn't derived from the basic MBTI instrument. The instrument uses forced-choice bi-modal questions.

---

10 Carl G. Jung, Psychological types, Routledge & Kegan Paul, 1971.

It's important to remember that this type of research originates from Anglo-Saxon or North American thinking and has been exported worldwide. However, by incorporating other types of logic, such as Ying-yang or Taoism, we can realise that basing profiling on bi-modal dimensions is limiting. We should apply this thinking and new logic to the scales of Myers-Briggs.

To determine the preference for thinking or feeling, a forced choice question like the following is typically asked:

(a)  I like to subject a problem to rational thought and logical analysis. Wishing something were true, does not make it so. Feelings are not 'wrong'. They're irrelevant.

(b)  I always ask myself what I feel about a problem, because 'the heart has its own reasons which Reason knows not of'. I seek to develop emotional muscles.

Thus, with a series of such questions, we are trying to place the individual along the scale such as in Fig. 1.

The way a person answers this question can reveal valuable insights about the dominant culture they operate in, as it may prefer decisive action or consultation (as was originally intended when MBTI was developed). However, in a multi-cultural environment, there may be individuals with differing opinions. A decisive leader may struggle when faced with the desire for consensus, while a sensitive leader may appear indecisive. This creates a dilemma between the seemingly opposing orientations of Thinking and Feeling.

Our colleague Charles Hampden-Turner (2001)[11] proposed a solution to this dilemma through their meta-level Dilemma Theory. By introducing two alternative options, we can better assess an individual's ability to reconcile this conflict:

(c)  I like to subject a problem to rational thought and logical analysis. Yet feats of intelligence or folly arouse feelings within me, so these too guide my intelligence.

(d)  I always ask myself what I feel about a problem because my boredom, irritation, or excitement is an early clue to whether I can engage intelligently and find a solution.

**Fig. 1.  Example Linear Scale.**

---

11 Private communication from Charles Hampden-Turner 001.

If you choose option (c), you will start by thinking about things while also considering other people's feelings. This brings together opposites in a successful way. Through a spiralling motion from one axis to the top right location (10, 10), the individual has integrated both elements as illustrated in Fig. 2.

Similar to those who responded with (a), those who responded with a (d) began from 'feeling' but moved towards 'thinking' and again integrated the two seemingly incompatible orientations shown in Fig. 3.

We can take preference between judging and perceiving as a second example: Traditionally, instruments ask questions like the following:

While tackling an issue I rather work in a ...

(a) structured and organised way,

(b) flexible way, with the necessary improvisation.

There is a propensity in Germany to score higher on (a) when (b) would rather target the French audience. Therefore, wouldn't the following be a more

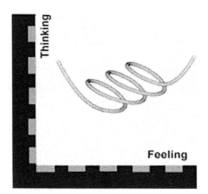

**Fig. 2.   From Thinking to Feeling.**

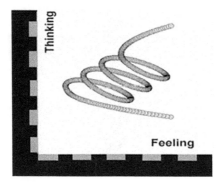

**Fig. 3.   From Feeling to Thinking.**

effective way to diagnose effective orientations in a team or group that included both Germans and Latinos?

(c) structured way in order to stimulate improvisation in certain boundaries,

(d) way with the necessary improvisation trying to develop the best procedures and organisation.

The two extreme opposite values for each conjugate pair are represented by our own questions in our enlarged MBTI model, which we refer to as the ITI (Integrated Type Indicator) see Fig. 4. However, we also include two more options that stand for the reconciliation of these opposites in a clockwise and an anticlockwise direction.

Our resulting ITI profile that shows the level to which an answer to a set of questions in this extended style is accurate by integrating the responses. For each variable, the sum of the answers to these extended questions yields a scale from 0 to 10. Then the overall propensity to reconcile (= an index between 0 and 100) is:

(Introvert + Extrovert) + (Sensing + Intuiting) + (Thinking + Feeling) + (Judging + Perceiving) ÷ 4 = **Developing Creativity Potential**

Responses to this ITI model's online web-based iteration have been examined. This model has already produced insights above and above the fundamental MBTI profile based on the conventional four linear scales when taken alone, that is, responses to this instrument alone.

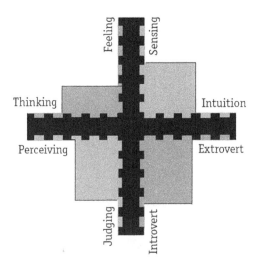

**Fig. 4. ITI Profile.**

We can assess an individual's capacity for problem-solving as a direct indicator of creativity using the integrated approach. We call this inventive competence. It is independent of the particular culture in which it can be measured, making it a reliable, universal model. The true core of the creative person is reconciliation.

This ITI is different because it is underpinned by the recognition that, while managers work to accomplish this or that separate objective, creative leaders deal with the dilemmas of seemingly 'opposed' objectives, which they continually seek to reconcile. Given the importance of reconciling opposites, it is surprising that no instrument that measures this has been published before.

Published models of creativity tend to lack a coherent, underlying rationale or proposition that predicts effective innovative behaviours. These models tend to seek the same end but through different approaches.

These lists are only guidelines, like a recipe's ingredients, and do not provide a holistic understanding of the experience. This can be confusing for innovative leaders who must decide which approach to follow and whether to adopt their own or foreign cultural values. Creativity theories mostly come from English-speaking countries, which could lead to ethnocentric thinking. It's unclear how applicable these lists are to other cultures and whether different styles are necessary. Richard Branson is an example of a leader who can reconcile opposing perspectives and switch between roles. It's important to be aware of potential limitations when applying linear models across international boundaries but combining different orientations can help leaders thrive in diversity.

No one has ever measured this skill in us.

## 2.3. RE-EXAMINING LEARNING STYLES

Kolb[12] offers one of the most helpful descriptive models of the adult learning process that is now available. Kolb was inspired by Kurt Lewin's work.[13]

According to Kolb's model, there are four stages that occur one after the other. The first is concrete experience, which is followed by reflection on the experience (reflective observation). The application of established theories or general principles may then come next (abstract conceptualisation), and after

---

12 Kolb, D., Learning style inventory, Boston, MA: McBer and Company, 1985.

13 Lewin, K. (1942). Field theory and learning. In Cartwright, D. (ed.), Field theory in social science: selected theoretical papers, London: Social Science Paperbacks, 1951.

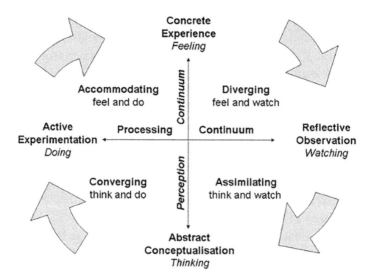

**Fig. 5.   Kolb Learning Cycle.**

that, the alteration of the subsequent occurrence of the experience (active experimentation), which in turn results in the subsequent concrete experience.

According to Kolb's model (Fig. 5), abstract conceptualisation and real experience are also diametrically opposed modes, as are active exploration and contemplative observation. The following four learning style types can be defined by combining or crossing the four learning modes:

- Divergers – reflective observation combined with concrete experience.

- Assimilators – reflective observation combined with abstract conceptualisation.

- Convergers – active experimentation combined with abstract conceptualisation.

- Accommodators – active experimentation combined with concrete experience.

Hudson[14] was the first to draw this distinction between types of knowledge and thinking methods.

---

14 Hudson, L., Contrary imaginations; A psychological study of the English school-
   boy, Harmondsworth: Penguin.

## 2.3.1. Creativity and Learning Styles

According to Kolb, those who practice creative disciplines, like the arts, are located in the divergent quadrant; those who work in practical sciences and law are located in the convergent quadrant; and those who must use their intuition more, like instructors, are located in the accommodative quadrant. Within the more general disciplines, there are also variations in where the specialists are located.

The whole creative process, according to our research, involves bringing together the opposites, that is, active experimentation and introspective observation, as well as real experience and abstract conceptualisation. Again, creativity flourishes where opposites converge.

Donald Schön refers to the fusion of theory and practice as The Reflective Practitioner.[15] Through Schön's work, educators have become accustomed to the idea of reflective practice.

This idea has a historical foundation in the learning tradition supported by Dewey, Lewin, and Piaget. They believed that learning relies on integrating experience with reflection and theory with practice. Reflection is essential for learning, as it enables critical analysis of one's actions to improve professional practice. However, is it necessary for creativity? According to Schön, reflection is required when unexpected outcomes occur during an activity, which he refers to as 'knowing-in-action'. To be innovative, the reflective practitioner needs to balance active experimentation with reflective observation and integrate abstractions with specific experiences.

Schön identified two types of reflection: reflection *on* action, which occurs after or during an activity, and reflection in action, which occurs during an activity without interrupting it. Reflection *in* action allows professionals to become researchers in the context of practice, enabling them to develop new theories to fit unique situations.

Reflective practice enhances the ability to articulate tacit knowledge, which is essential for sharing professional skills and enhancing professional knowledge and practice. Reflective practice has advantages and disadvantages, as it can positively affect professional growth and development but is time-consuming and may involve personal risk. Professionals should first recognise and apply standard practice rules and techniques before developing and testing new forms of understanding and action.

The reflective practitioner (as illustrated in Fig. 6) should reconcile active experimentation with reflective observation and integrate abstractions with

---

15 D.A. Schön, The reflective practitioner, New York: Basic Books, 1983 and D.A. Schön, Educating the reflective practitioner, San Francisco: Jossey-Bass, 1988.

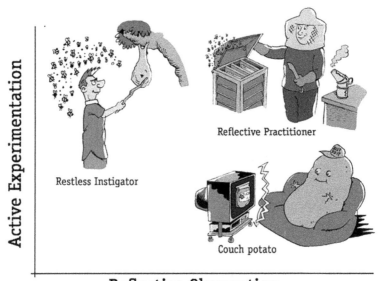

Fig. 6.  **The Reflective Practitioner.**

concrete experiences to be creative and avoid repeating mistakes. Finally, the creative process requires starting with a concrete experience, considering potential outcomes, and using alternative question formats, investigating levels of reconciliation, *and rejecting linear models.*

## 2.4. THE ADAPTOR-INNOVATOR CONSTRUCT

Individual problem-solving and problem-definition approaches are evaluated using Kirton's[16] KAI. In this context, 'style' refers to a problem-solving approach that is more adaptable, developmental, or analogic as opposed to inventive or ground-breaking.

Kirton's KAI measures individual styles of problem definition and solving. Style, in this case, refers to an adaptive, building, or analogic problem-solving style versus an innovative or pioneering style. Kirton argues that:

> Adaptation-Innovation theory is located in the domain of cognitive function, specifically part of the strategic stable characteristic preferred style that people seek to bring about intended change ...

---

16 M.J. Kirton (ed.), Adaptors and innovators: styles of creativity and problem solving, revised edition, New York: Routledge, 1994.

there is a sharp distinction between style and the capacity or level of cognition of which a person is capable, whether this is inherent or learned. The latter describes the 'power of the engine'; the former the 'manner in which it is driven'.

Jack Hipple[17] et al. provided a summary of the two groupings and how each group is perceived by its antagonists in Table 2.

Kirton observed that while some managers were successful in bringing about change that enhanced the existing system, they failed to recognise opportunities that existed outside the parameters of the system.[18] Kirton refers to this fashion as 'adaptive'. Other managers were adept at coming up with ideas that brought about more dramatic transformation, but they struggled to win support for their radical suggestions. This fashion was dubbed 'innovative' by Kirton. These findings led Kirton[19] to propose the adaptor-innovator personality continuum, which assumes two radically different ways of approaching innovative change.

Perhaps their clarity and precision are Kirton's assumptions' greatest flaws. One of the fundamental presumptions is that cognitive style, which forms the

**Table 2. Adaptors Versus Innovators.**

| Adaptors | Innovators |
| --- | --- |
| Efficient, thorough, adaptable, methodical, organised, precise, reliable, dependable | Ingenious, original, independent, unconventional |
| Accepts problem definition | Challenges problem definition |
| Concerned with resolving problems rather than finding them | Discovers problems and avenues for their solutions |
| Seeks solutions to problems in tried and understood ways | Manipulates problems by questioning existing assumptions |
| Reduces problems by improvement and greater efficiency, while aiming at continuity and stability | Is a catalyst to unsettled groups, irreverent of their consensual views |
| Seems impervious to boredom; able to maintain high accuracy in long spells of detailed work | Capable of routine work (system maintenance) for only short bursts; quick to delegate routine tasks |
| Is an authority within established structures | Tends to take control in unstructured situations |

17 Jack Hipple (et al). 'Can corporate innovation champions survive?', Chemical Innovation Magazine 31, No. 11, pp. 14. 22, November 2001.

18 Kirton, M. J., Management initiative, London: Acton Society Trust, 1961.

19 Kirton, M. J., 'Adaptors and innovators: a description of a measure', Journal of Applied Psychology 61, 1976.

basis of the KAI instrument, is conceptually independent of cognitive ability, success, cognitive strategies, and coping behaviour. We agree, but this is all predicated on Kirton's more oblique assertion that the innovator and adaptor styles are antagonistic to one another.

A greater score on the adaptor side (see Fig. 7) naturally results in a lower score on the innovator side, as is effectively demonstrated by the presentation of the KAI instrument's scores as the scores on a balance. As we said earlier, people have two hands, but they prefer to write with only one, therefore much like the MBTI, the main focus is on the preferences that people have.

Again, we have the issue of a linear scale, which doesn't provide for any way to investigate if or how respondents can use their adaptive orientation to strengthen their innovator orientation.

## 2.5. OUR INTEGRATED TYPE INDICATOR (ITI)

To explore the concept of a non-linear scale, we requested (initially) about 250 managers from a variety of cultural backgrounds to complete our ITI – being a modified version of the KAI in order to give empirical support for these bold assertions.

We discovered that innovators extrovertly disclose their introverted calculation, constantly learn by swinging between judging and perceiving, and finally check their feelings through thinking. Creative persons also found to move more efficiently between intuition and thinking. Another finding is that responders' starting points are frequently influenced by their culture. Therefore, we do not claim that one culture is more creative than another; rather, we claim that each culture approaches problems from a unique starting point. Lack of inventiveness can be shown in the failure to combine opposing logics. One-handed clapping produces little sound.

So, as opposed to Kirton's original KAI's questions, which are based on linear (Likert) scales, our 'integrated innovation indicator' poses the following kinds of inquiries.

Range of participant scores from Adapter
through to highly Creative Inventor

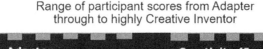

**Fig. 7.  Kirton's Linear Scale.**

*Note to reader*: while Kirton uses the terms 'adapter' and 'innovator', for reasons explained below, we replace his use of 'innovator' by the term 'inventor'. We reserve the use of the term 'innovator' as the combination (reconciliation) of adapting and inventing.

*Q1 example*: Which of the following four statements most accurately sums up your typical behaviour?

(a) I am reliable, dependable, thorough, methodical, organised, and efficient (5 points for invention, 0 points for adaptation, and 0 points for innovation).

(b) I have intelligence, originality, independence, and am unpredictable (0 points for invention, 5 points for adaptation, and 0 points for innovation).

(c) I consistently test whether my initial ideas actually function in practice in an organised and thorough way (5 points for invention, 0 points for adaptation, and 9 points for innovation).

(d) In order to lay the groundwork for my unique thoughts, I am meticulous and organised first (0 points for invention, 5 points for adaptation, and 9 points for innovation).

*Q2 example*: Which of the following four options best describes you?

(a) I tend to be concerned with resolving problems rather than finding them (5 score in invention, 0 score in adaptation, 0 score on innovation).

(b) I tend to discover problems and avenues for their solutions (0 score in invention, 5 score in adaptation, 0 score on innovation).

(c) I tend to look for redefining problems by trial and error after I have tried to solve the existing problems first (5 score in invention, 0 score in adaptation, 9 score on innovation).

(d) I tend to look for conventional methods of solving problems only after I have discovered all the possible problems and avenues for their solutions (0 score in invention, 5 score in adaptation, 9 score on innovation).

Our research data indicate that when faced with the choice between type (a) and type (b) options for invention and adaptation, people tend to prefer one over the other. However, when we add options (c) and (d) that combine both approaches, they can give us a score on our innovation index. To better understand the innovative style, we can view it as a reconciliation between the adaptor and inventive styles. Figs. 8 and 9 depict this dilemma with further example question statements.

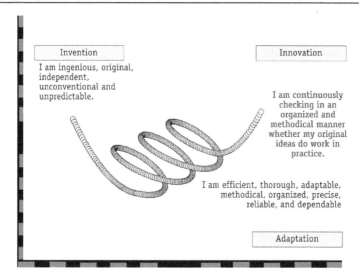

**Fig. 8.**   **From Invention Through Adaption to Innovation.**

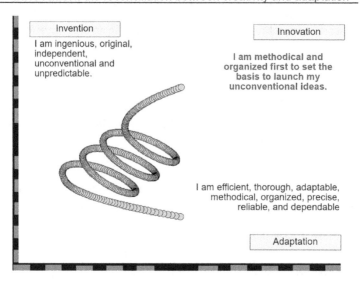

**Fig. 9.**   **From Adaptation Through Invention to Innovation.**

## 2.6. HUMOUR AND ORIGINALITY

When looking for innovative new ideas, many of us fall into the same trap. Looking at the creative process implies that we should do the opposite and roll up our sleeves and say, 'It's time to go and play', as opposed to rolling up our sleeves and saying, 'It's time to get to work'.

Here are just a few of the ways that humour and/or play can stimulate original thought:

1. Humour and creativity both involve experimenting with concepts and shifting our viewpoints.

2. Play truly provides an energetic feeling that charges the neurons and puts them ready for action, using another section of our brains (laughing increases the level of adrenaline and oxygen going to the brain).

3. Play reduces our inhibitions, making it less likely that we will stifle truly new thoughts.

4. In the workplace, humour encourages a culture of taking risks, which is a crucial component.

5. Humour questions our fundamental presumptions and norms.

6. Play promotes spontaneity, which is essential for coming up with original ideas.

7. Humour encourages brainstorming rather than 'blame-storming', which keeps people's attention on solutions.

Humour and creativity are interchangeable. Both of these require establishing a connection between two disparate elements by combining them. This fundamental contrast may be seen in a few scenes from some of the more well-known comedies.

Comedy writers like John Cleese (Monty Python, Fawlty Towers), John Sullivan (Only Fools and Horses), and Matt Groening (The Simpsons) produce work that is very different from ours yet complements it. We seem to share the same trait of using humour in a practical way. They all share Arthur Koestler's view that humour and creativity are closely related. Why? Because learning that two seemingly incompatible logics are actually both rational is the process of humour. What makes you chuckle is that, as Koestler has demonstrated, humour is based on bi-sociation,[20] which is the capacity to intellectually and

---

20 Arthur Koestler, The act of creation, Penguin (Non-Classics), Reissue edition, 5 June 1990.

emotionally travel both directions of a diverging train of thought and which, when recognised, causes laughing. Humour-based bi-sociation gives managers a more nuanced perspective on their company since it offers an and/and orientation to the tensions between managing and organising rather than an either/or perspective.

This cannot be done with linear thinking and the necessity to be mistake-free a priori, according to the results of our study. The (commercial) world we live in begins to be burdened with conundrums that cannot be ignored by making linear decisions if we appreciate the diversity of the human species and its cultures. To resolve these problems, an alternate, non-linear technique is required. Humour is simply one successful strategy for dealing with problems. Always two opposite methods to screw up are available. Just make a joke, and let's try again.

Arthur Koestler believed that humour can be the starting point for creativity. Humorous situations often involve conflicting ideas that collide with each other, creating a logical unfolding that we can all follow. For example, when a man makes advances towards a woman who declines, he may respond by saying, 'I wasn't aiming that high'. The word 'high' can refer to both the nobility of his feelings and the woman's physical features, creating a double meaning that surprises us and makes us laugh.

However, for humour to be truly creative, it must go beyond mere gags and become something larger. It must fuse together different frames of reference to create a deeper meaning. John Cleese's 'The Psychiatrist' accomplishes this by providing insights into the human condition and the struggles of those who try to uphold morality.

In 'Faulty Towers', Basil's hang-ups are dissected with a sharp blade. It's important that the audience doesn't sympathise with Basil, as his misfortunes are often self-inflicted. Instead, we take joy in seeing his killjoy antics lead to his defeat. Basil's struggles represent a rear-guard action against the breakdown of class barriers, the acceptance of eroticism, the tolerance of bad service, and the growing culture of spin that we see today.

## 2.7. NEURO-LINGUISTIC PROGRAMMING

Are there numerous ways that people can be creative, or is there a single, universal method?

Natural Language Processing (NLP) has emerged as a fascinating field for exploring the intersection of language and creativity. NLP techniques can be used to enhance and even inspire creative processes, such as generating original content, artistic expressions, and innovative ideas. Here is a brief overview with reference to explore the connection between NLP and creativity:

*Text Generation and Storytelling*: NLP models, like OpenAI's GPT-3, have advanced the capabilities of text generation. They can be trained on vast amounts of text data to automatically generate coherent and contextually relevant stories, poetry, and even dialogue. This technology opens up new possibilities for creative writing and storytelling. Brown[21] et al. (2020) revealed the potential of GPT-3 for various creative applications, showcasing its ability to generate a wide range of texts.

*Creative Dialogue and Conversational Agents*: NLP models can be used to create conversational agents or chatbots that engage in dynamic and creative interactions with users. These chatbots can generate witty responses, tell jokes, or engage in imaginative conversations. Li[22] et al. (2016) explored the use of NLP in developing creative chatbots that actively participate in collaborative storytelling.

*Language-based Creative Tasks*: NLP models can assist in diverse language-based creative tasks. This includes generating poetry, writing lyrics, composing music, and even creating visual art descriptions. For instance, Huang[23] et al. (2020) developed an NLP model capable of generating novel Chinese poetry.

*Idea Generation and Innovation*: NLP techniques, such as topic modelling and sentient analysis, can be used to analyse vast amounts of text data to identify emerging trends, patterns, and insights. This assists in idea generation and innovation by revealing underlying themes or providing inspiration for novel solutions. Yi[24] et al. (2019) demonstrated the potential of NLP in uncovering latent patterns for ideation and innovation.

*Personalised Recommendations and Creative Discoveries*: NLP-based recommendation systems help users discover creative content tailored to their preferences. By analysing user preferences and behaviour, NLP models can provide personalised suggestions for books, movies, music, and other artistic expressions. These recommendations can lead to serendipitous discoveries and inspire individuals in their own creative endeavours.

21 Brown, T. B., et al. (2020). Language models are few-shot learners. arXiv preprint arXiv:2005.14165.

22 Li, J., et al. (2016). A persona-based neural conversation model. Proceedings of the 54th Annual Meeting of the Association for Computational Linguistics (ACL).

23 Huang, M., et al. (2020). Improved poem generation with external common-sense knowledge. In The Thirty-Fourth AAAI Conference on Artificial Intelligence (AAAI-20).

24 Yi, S., et al., 'Unveiling the patterns of innovation: A topic modelling approach', Technological Forecasting and Social Change 148, 119712, 2019.

Initially, proponents of NLP taught that most people preferred to process information predominantly in one sense and had internal preferred representational systems (PRS).

Some people tell how they 'saw' an idea in their heads since they tend to be more visually inclined. Others recall sounds or whispers they 'heard' in their heads that gave them the original thought. Some people can 'feel' or 'touch' a concept because they are predominantly kinaesthetic.

## VIGNETTE: AFTER THE PHD VIVA EXAMINATION

Author Peter has been involved as both examiner and supervisor in many PhD viva voce examinations. He always had a friendly follow-up chat after the examination once they left the examination room. He recalls particularly how different students responded to a common question he asked them:

About a half would answer, 'I **see** what you mean'

About a quarter would answer, 'I **hear** what you say'

The remainder variously said, 'I really **felt** it'

Even the gustatory can have a taste in their mouth when inventing, and some people can even olfactory (literally) 'smell' an idea. Practitioners of NLP have long noticed that different people express their creativity in different ways by using their senses, but this may not always imply that they do so in a hair-brain mode. Beethoven's hearing loss made it difficult for him to play the piano properly, but it had no effect on his inventiveness. Beethoven composed nine symphonies between 1800 and 1824, many of which are today regarded as masterpieces. In 1804, at the time he finished writing his third symphony, the Eroica, he became entirely deaf.

Practitioners of NLP contend that you should pay attention to the person you are speaking with in order to ascertain their preferences. Then give up your own preferred orientation and embrace your business partner's inclinations. But in our opinion, this is equivalent to attempting to impress a date by acting out of character. The potential of creativity that draws from and combines all the senses is much greater.

## 2.8. HBDI AND CEREBRAL DOMINANCE

In the 1970s, Ned Herrmann started to create the HBDITM and Whole Brain Thinking discourse. The specialised nature of the human brain has long been known. The specialised modes of the brain are divided up into one or more of these four physiological structures according to his whole brain theory. The four quadrant model is built on this distribution of specialised modes. We now have the foundation for a far more complex and helpful model that includes not only the left and right modes but also the cerebral and limbic modes because dominance can only occur between paired structures. The limbic mode is made up of the two interrelated halves of the limbic system, whereas the cerebral modes are made up of the two interconnected cerebral hemispheres. Numerous studies have revealed that there are just as many people with predominately cerebral or limbic mental preferences as there are with predominately left or right mental preferences.

Therefore, the four-quadrant whole brain model (HBDI profile – see Fig. 10) enables us to distinguish between visceral, structured, and emotional, which represent limbic preferences, as well as the more advanced conceptions of cognitive and intellectual, which describe the cerebral choice. Hermann contends that after knowing their HBDI profile, an individual or group is better equipped to successfully use their understanding of their preferred learning, communicating, and problem-solving styles, leading to increased creativity and effectiveness.

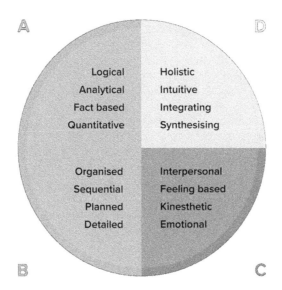

**Fig. 10.  HBDI Model Profile.**

The ability to be creative, however, doesn't seem to be associated with any particular HBDI profile.

But once more, we contend that creativity is the outcome of the combination of the cognitive and limbic, the logical analytic with the more emotive quadrants. Although people may start out with varied preferences or orientations, it is how well they connect these orientations that leads to innovative thinking.

## 2.9. INDIVIDUAL CREATIVITY – INITIAL SUMMARY

We have made an effort to demonstrate that despite the abundance of models and frameworks available for examining individual creativity, the focus is still on reductionism, most likely as a result of an excess of Anglo-Saxon or US linear (Cartesian) thinking and research.

In essence, the creative process is a process where several logics come together to produce a new reality. If we take a closer look at the Japanese garden, we can observe that it serves as an invitation to gather various points of view, making each visit an artistic endeavour. And when we walk together, your point of view and mine are connected.

The remainder of this book will continue this journey.

# 3

# CREATIVITY IN TEAMS

Does collaboration among creative individuals ensure that teams and organisations grow more innovative?

The extant research is contradictory and open to interpretation, yet it repeatedly demonstrates that diversity is essential for a team to be inventive. Executives in human resources see improved talent utilisation, market insight, as well as higher creativity and problem-solving skills as the main benefits of greater workplace diversity.[1]

Reviewing nearly 50 years of social science research on diversity in teams, however, makes the situation seem lot less clear-cut. A group's capacity to function effectively is more likely to be negatively impacted by obvious distinctions, such as those of race/ethnicity, gender, or age, according to Elizabeth Mannix[2] and Margaret Lean, who have made an effort to separate what researchers have discovered over the past 50 years. Contrarily, fundamental distinctions, like those in functional background, educational attainment, or personality, frequently result in performance improvement. Underlying differences, in particular, can encourage innovation or team problem-solving, but once again, only when the group process is carefully supported.

Hoffman found in some early research that heterogeneous groups were better at coming up with solutions to complicated decision-making situations than homogenous groups. In contrast to homogeneous groupings of like-minded

---

1   Gail Robinson and Kathleen Dechant, "Building a business case for diversity", The Academy of Management Executive (1993–2005), Vol. 11, No. 3 (August, 1997), pp. 21–31.

2   E. The Mannix and M. Lean, "Diverse teams in organizations," American Psychological Society, 2005, Psychological science in the public interest, Volume 6: Number 2.

people, he said that varied groups of people should be expected to have a wider range of information, expertise, and opinions. These elements ought to encourage more productive group performance, particularly when the activity is cognitively challenging or necessitates multiple viewpoints.[3] However, according to some research, the business case for diversity (in terms of measurable, 'black and white' financial results) is still difficult to make.[4] These latter studies, however, lack a comprehensive or long-term viewpoint and are all based on general research.

## 3.1. FOSTERING INNOVATION IN A TEAM

A critical review of published research shows that when teams combine three key elements, they are more innovative:

1. they are diverse;

2. they are inclusive and exchange information and expertise; and

3. they support the fundamental enabling procedures, particularly leadership.

Triandis[5] and colleagues conducted an early line of research on diversity and problem-solving techniques. They explicitly emphasised that difficult jobs requiring inventiveness benefitted most from diversity.

When we examine critically what kind of diversity fosters innovation in teams, we find that it is the invisible traits that predominate. Functional variations in knowledge, ability, and expertise in particular have been found to enhance performance because they spark enlightening debate, which promotes innovation and better problem resolution. These results support the idea that diversity in teams fosters constructive disagreement, resulting in higher-level outcomes than would be possible in teams with a greater degree of homogeneity. In this chapter's conceptual framework, we define these phenomena as the resolution of conflicts brought about by various points of view. The tensions resulting from these conundrums serve as the primary catalyst for creativity.

---

3  L. Richard Hoffman and Norman R. F. Maier, "Quality and acceptance of problem solutions by members of homogeneous and heterogeneous groups," Journal of Abnormal and Social Psychology, Vol. 62, No. 2, pp. 401–407, 1961.

4  Levine, D., Joshi, A., Jehn, K., Leonard, J., Kochan, T., Bezrukova, K., Ely, R., Jackson, S. The effects of diversity on business: Report of the diversity research network. Human Resource Management, Vol. 42, No. 1, pp. 3–21.

5  Triandis, H. C. (1994). Culture and social behavior. New York, NY: McGraw-Hill.

Resolving these conundrums is the key problem, and as such, it calls for the competency of a team leader.[6]

The world has been changed by little groups, according to Margaret Mead.[7] The success of an organisation is most heavily influenced by the leadership and team dynamics as well as the interactions between all team members. In fact, nothing else ever has.

## 3.2. TEAM ROLES

The British novelist and consultant Meredith Belbin is ascribed to be one of the management teams' most creative thinkers. In his first book,[8] he details how one Apollo Team, which was made up of very skilled individuals, performed substantially worse than a second Apollo Team, which was made up of individuals who were far less talented but who worked well together. According to Belbin, a successful team consists of individuals who work towards a common objective while moving through the four stages of forming, storming, norming, and performing. Belbin argues that the performance of teams and therefore its innovative power is dependent on the diversity of roles that its incumbents play. He distinguished nine such roles:

1. The Plant: This is the ideas-generator and originator of the team's creative potential. S/he 'thinks out of the box'.

2. The Shaper: The Shaper gets people to shape up around the new idea and drives the idea through. S/he is sometimes called the Product Champion and puts momentum behind the idea.

3. The Resource Investigator: This is a person whose role is to spot opportunities, as well as mobilise the resources necessary to carry through the project. Windows of Opportunity may open very briefly and must be darted through.

4. The Coordinator: The responsibility of this role is to 'open the gate' allowing the ideas into the team, co-ordinating and repairing the team as it digests

---

6  Carpenter, 2002; Pitcher and Smith, 2000; and Bunderson and Sutcliffe, 2002.

7  Never doubt that a small group of thoughtful, committed citizens can change the world. Indeed, it's the only thing that ever has – Margaret Mead Paperback – 26 June 2019, by Mickey's Journals (Author).

8  Meredith Belbin, Management Teams: Why they succeed or fail, by, Butterworth Heinemann, 1981 (2ed. 1993).

the new ideas. New ideas are potentially disintegrative so restoring team cohesion can be vital.

5. The Expert: This is the expert in some key discipline essential to the project/ product, for example, the electronics engineer or tool-maker. Without technical brilliance, the entire project may fail to match standards or specifications.

6. The Monitor Evaluator: This is the role of a critic, who kills ideas that are wasting the team's time, but constructively improves ideas and implementations that require further work and elaboration. The Monitor Evaluator is often very intelligent and sceptical.

7. The Implementer: The Implementer is the person who gives the idea its embodiment as a product or services, who makes an ideal real and gives to some vision a practical utility.

8. The Completer Finisher: This role 'edits' the finished project/product and refines it for customer use. The Completer Finisher is a 'detail person' and takes infinite pains to get the whole system user-friendly.

9. The Team Worker: This role is for the socio-emotional specialist who maintains the morale and the cohesion of the team by healing any hurts. S/he encourages participation, facilitates team processes and may even do running repairs on gaps or splits in the team. The best team workers sense any incompleteness and supply the needed roles.

Conventional wisdom purports that a team needs each of these roles to be effective. Not just nine team members, but the available team members contributing through their primary and secondary roles. When putting a team together, it may be part of the strategy for selection to ensure all team roles will be present. But in practice, teams may be the mix of people already in post with one or more team roles absent. Belbin's original model didn't consider the personality conflicts between extreme roles – such as the tensions between those offering creative ideas and those concerned with practical issues of implementation.

Originally, our interest in teams was our research on cross-cultural teams and to extend Belbin's work develop a broad theory that contends that conflicts between the major positions in a team contribute to innovation. The process of turning ideas into actual products or projects is hampered if any of these positions are absent or inadequately filled. We no longer limit our attention to the role of 'the Plant', or the group member who generates new ideas. Here, we concentrate on scenarios in which the Plant's ideas have widespread support from other roles; as a result, we anticipate that the team will be successful in generating new ideas.

When it comes to entrepreneurship, the sole founder of a business must either assume all necessary duties themselves or hire others to do so. In any case, the founder must assume responsibility for ensuring that these duties are fulfilled, or else the entire business could fail.

We can understand why a team is, or is not, good at innovation by examining the tensions between team responsibilities since a diversity of roles is essential to any and every inventive teamwork. Additionally, we can 'map' these conflicts so that teams may assess their situation and, if necessary, take remedial action by bolstering the underperforming roles.

## 3.3. PHASES OF CREATIVITY AND CONFLICT BETWEEN TEAM ROLES

In order to effectively manage innovation within a team, it is not enough to simply assign different roles at varying intensities during different stages. It is also important to address and reconcile the conflicts that arise between these roles. We need to explore five key stages of a new-product project and the common dilemmas that arise between the various team roles at each stage. While there are certainly other conflicts that can arise throughout the process, these examples will help illustrate how to manage them as they arise.

The five key stages are as follows:

Stage 1 – Scoping: This is a brief and inexpensive assessment of the project's technical merit and market potential.

Stage 2 – Building the business case: This is a crucial stage in which technical, marketing, and business feasibility are assessed. The result is a business case consisting of three main components: project and product definition, project justification, and project plan.

Stage 3 – Development: During this stage, the plans outlined in the business case are translated into concrete deliverables. The product is developed, the manufacturing or operations plan is mapped out, the marketing launch and operating plans are developed, and test plans for the next stage are defined.

Stage 4 – Testing and validation: This stage is designed to validate the entire project, including the product itself, the production process, customer acceptance, and the project's economics.

Stage 5 – Launch: This is the final stage, during which the product is fully commercialised and production and commercial launch begin.

Throughout these stages, there are five frequently recurring conflicts that can arise between team roles. While there are certainly other conflicts that can arise, these five are we continued to observe:

- Goal alignment.

- Role clarity.

- Resource allocation.

- Communication and collaboration.

- Decision-making authority.

It is important to address these conflicts as they arise in order to ensure a successful outcome for the team's delivery.

These five 'crises' represent important tensions at the quantum gates that are a part of the creative process (as shown in Table 3). Making sure that each role successfully interacts with its antagonist is the challenge. Successful innovation will come once all of these issues have been overcome.

In order to explain the model of the reconciliation process and how it supports a team's creativity, we will now examine one of these conundrums.

### 3.3.1. Creative Ideas Versus Critical Appraisal in Stage 1 Scoping

> 'a quick and affordable evaluation of the project's technical viability and business potential.'

Although there is little evidence that having more than one Plant makes the team more creative, the Plant or creative individual must be on the team.

---

**Table 3. Tensions Between Team Roles.**

| The Tension Expressed as a Dilemma | Role Versus Role | |
|---|---|---|
| 1   *Scoping:* Creative Ideas versus Critical Appraisal | Plant | Monitor Evaluator |
| 2   *Build business case:* Real versus Window of Opportunity | Resource Investigator | Shaper |
| 3   *Development:* Disciplines versus Final Alignment. | Specialist | Coordinator |
| 4   *Testing and validation* Consensus versus Mature | Team Worker | Completer Finisher |
| 5   *Launch:* Capturing Resources versus Practical Embodiment | Resource Investigator | Implementer |

The team needs diversity in all roles. Major flaws arise if not all or the majority of the positions are filled. No matter how creative the discourse, having three, four, or five people talking at once without nobody listening or taking anything on board is a formula for team sterility. Having merely plants, however, will result in concepts that aren't tested; these ideas must be analysed in order to determine the project's viability.

> The interaction between creativity and critique is arguably more important to innovation than anything else. Critique can boost imagination, allowing perfection to emerge from the 'purging fires'. Brilliant artists are portrayed as starving in garrets because critics can't or won't recognise their brilliance. However, the critic receives a terrible rap: 'No statue was ever raised to a critic'.

### 3.3.2. Mapping the Three Types of Failure

> Consider the Dilemma Grid. Without creative ideas, which are located on the horizontal axis, innovation is impossible. Without Critical Appraisal, time would be squandered endlessly on unsound theories, which is shown by the vertical axis. Most creative work that defies or avoids critique is Blue Sky (grid reference 1/10), which is too speculative, long-term, and idealistic for anyone to be tempted to approach it critically. Why bother if it's merely an idea?

> However, many concepts are strangled at Birth when reviewers go on the rampage or the team is overrun with Monitor Evaluators (10/1). What better way to demonstrate your critical faculties to the Monitor Evaluator, who is frequently a very clever person, than to take a fledgling concept and destroy it? It should be sufficient to simply list all the obstacles in the way of its achievement (see Fig. 11).

> You barely allow it to emerge from the ground before you throttle it. Grudging acceptance (5/5) is also inadequate because it just represents a compromise.

### 3.3.3. Tracing the Resolution

Ideas quickly become scarce. Ideas may nonetheless have a Short Life even though detractors are less damaging (5/5). If they don't pass away right away, they might pass away during the development, manufacturing, marketing, etc.

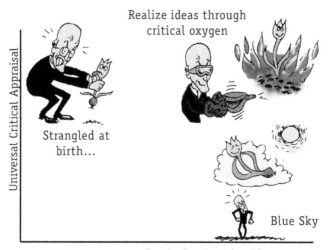

Fig. 11. Tensions Between Ideas and Critical Appraisal.

stages, especially if they have to bear the price of expanding their distribution options. EMI's Magnetic Resonance Scanner[9] won a Nobel Prize, but the company lost $300 million by selling it to hospitals rather than music stores. Less than 10% of registered patents generate revenue. Perhaps there isn't enough (but also not enough!) criticism. Customers may be interested in things that are novel to them rather than those that are novel to science.

To innovate, ideas must be improved without being destroyed (although some ideas are non-viable, for unforeseeable reasons). Criticism must be positive and given with the intention of helping something or someone you admire improve. Like everyone else, the Plant makes mistakes and needs input to improve. In fact, doing something new makes you more likely to make mistakes, so constructive criticism from a trusted source is priceless. Similar minds have been stimulated during the great ages of creation, with participation from intelligent audiences, reviewers, sponsors, and patrons as well as artists. The Dadaists contested not only the traditional art of their criticising their own movement's members even more than their predecessors did, always aiming to get better.

We may follow the Creative Idea's development on the 'map' from its starting point (2/8), through a period of Critical Appraisal, back to a better product, then as it is dragged back into Critical Appraisal, until it emerges from the Refiner's Fire Constructively Improved.

---

9  Retrieved from Fig. 11 https://public.websites.umich.edu/~afuah/cases/case4. html.

## 3.4. THE COLLABORATIVE PROCESS

Positive criticism has unquestionable logic and power since it raises the like-lihood that potentially good ideas will be encouraged and terrible ideas will finally be killed. But how can we instil the team with such a spirit?

Synectics created a strategy that is incredibly effective. Anyone who wants to respond to a concept must first list at least three positive features of the proposal before expressing any potential criticism. Then, criticisms must be stated as follows: 'How can we get around the obstacle I see in implementing this innovation?'

So, rather than the Monitor Evaluator bringing up a suggestion and instantly killing it, the answer might be:

> 'I really appreciate the concept since it has the ability to attract
> a new clientele to our market'. Additionally, it demonstrates
> that we have another excellent product that would fit into our
> current distribution system. How can we obtain the extra funding
> and resources to support the market research, and what are the
> most cost-effective ways to assess the validity of this potential
> new product?

Rather than:

> 'Interesting idea, but I believe it will strain our resources too thin and
> waste our limited funds, moreover I doubt the product is trustworthy
> enough'.

Positive criticism, in fact, enhances the potential of the concept and hones your response to any potential flaws. The idea becomes clearer as a result. The fire of the team's innovative spirit is fuelled by criticism.

---

VIGNETTE: EXAMPLES FROM OUR WORKSHOP SESSIONS BASED
ON OUR RECONCILING APP.

Sheryl is a Shaper. She identified the dilemma she faced in working with the Finisher in her team and thought hard about how she could work better by reconciling this dilemma:

| Sheryl (Shaper) | | Other member (Finisher) |
| --- | --- | --- |
| Challenging, dynamic, thrives on pressure. The drive and courage to overcome obstacles. But prone to provocation. Offends people's feelings | Working with a contrasting team role | Painstaking, conscientious, anxious. Searches out errors and omissions. Delivers on time. But inclined to worry unduly. Reluctant to delegate |
| What Sheryl said about herself: 'difficult for me to take on and develop ideas I have not had an original input to' | | And about her colleague: 'May not appear interested in alternative viewpoints as focus is on detail and delivery' |
| What Sheryl proposed as a reconciliation | | |
| Request the finisher to structure meeting time to evaluate my new ideas and then to identify and discuss his concerns and how they could be overcome if my idea might be implemented | | |

Ralph is a Monitor Evaluator. He was aware of two dominant Plants in his team and wanted to find a solution to the challenges he faced in trying to work better with them

| Ralph (Monitor Evaluator) | | Other team members (Plants) |
| --- | --- | --- |
| Sober, strategic and discerning. Sees all options. Judges accurately. But lacks drive and ability to inspire others | Working with a contrasting team role | Creative, imaginative, unorthodox, solves difficult problems. But ignores incidentals. Too preoccupied to communicate effectively |
| What Ralph said about himself: 'I want to influence others to take action' | | And about his colleagues: 'Idea generation conflicts with need to meet deadlines and work with team' |
| What Ralph proposed as a reconciliation | | |

Create action plans with key deliverables with clear roles and responsibilities but which include specific tasks for the review of new ideas, their evaluation, and assessment of their implication

## 3.5. OUR ONLINE INVESTIGATIVE MODEL

We have used an interactive, web-based system to record the methods that help participants engage more effectively with other team roles as we have reproduced this expanded team role model with numerous client organisations. We are continually extending a database of inter and intra-team role dilemmas from these assessments, which describes all possible pairings of primary and opposing team roles. This growing database demonstrates that these conflicts are team-level expressions of the more general problems that affect organisations today. We also know from our work, where we assess how these reconciliations affect organisation operations, that this analysis enhances bottom-line business performance by fostering stronger teamwork.

Our own excessively created reconciliation profiles may help to explain why we have reservations about using any linear model across international boundaries. However, we firmly believe that a team can thrive in diversity by combining seemingly incompatible orientations. All team roles must be present and carried out, but the success of the team depends on how well they work together. Additionally, nothing like this has ever been measured before.

## 3.6. BIG CHIEF RECONCILER

We should be aware of the implicit values connected to the various roles in models like Belbin. Characteristics are frequently added to positions in most theoretical frameworks for team roles, as though they were stable and independent. However, in practice, how well a team utilises the distinctions in roles – where the dynamic of complementarities is crucial – determines its efficacy and capacity for innovation. The distinctions between each of the five phases' transitions, become even clearer, and the reconciliation of the different orientations becomes essential.

As roles become ever more obvious, it is crucial to reconcile the various orientations.

The main conflicts that arise between the various team positions must be resolved, and the relationship between the roles must be structured accordingly. The fundamental conditions for the team's success in this new mode of operation are safe, founded on a solid substructure, and prepared for nurturing.

People must work through their conflicts, and the Chair's role is to create a setting in the company where these conflicts can be resolved. The Chair's main responsibility at the meta-level is to resolve the conflict between the nomothetic (organisational perspective) and the idiographic (individual perspective of each employee) – that is, what is important to the team and what is important to the organisation.

To foster an environment where ideas are questioned, the Coordinator. There are no mistakes in a 'culture of invention'. When one person exhibits weakness, it triggers a cascade, allowing others to express their thoughts. People must complement one another. The Coordinator should also make the environment light hearted. 'I love laughter because then people can have new ideas', the Dalai Lama once said.

We would emphasise that the stereotyped team roles we discuss apply to the roles people play rather than to the individuals. People are much more flexible and complicated than this typological framework suggests, and they can play many different roles.

So, we can observe an executive who can perform all of these duties, but such a role model is uncommon. The majority of people do have a preference for certain roles over others. Any significant imbalance, such as a team with an excessive number of Monitor Evaluators or Specialists, causes a rapid decline in team performance. The Specialists struggle to communicate, and the Monitor Evaluators often interrupt one another. Even too many plants can result in verbal fireworks without any fruitful outcomes.

An idea originating with one or more Plants must be turned into a viable product or project by a Shaper and Implementer, while the Coordinator tries to align the necessary Specialists, Team Workers and other contributors. The resulting project is constructively criticised and improved by a Monitor Evaluator, before being readied for sale or presentation by the Completer Finisher. The Resource Investigator who earlier gathered the various resources needed, now matches the finished product with a window of opportunity in the environment. If there are any gaps in this process it is unlikely to have a successful outcome.

Note that the comic stereotypes are being applied to the roles people play, not the people themselves, who, being capable of taking on many roles are far more flexible and complex than this typology implies. An executive capable of playing all these roles is rare. Most people do have role preferences and much prefer some roles to others. Any serious imbalance, like a team with too many Monitor Evaluators or too many Specialists and team performance sharply deteriorates. The Monitor Evaluators cut each other down and the Specialists have difficulty communicating. There can even be too many Plants, with verbal fireworks but no useful conclusions.

Additionally, Belbin's research makes a compelling case for diversity. A team made up of diverse role-players works well because of how unique each one is. The described positions all complement one another, and authority should ideally change as the process progresses through different stages.

## 3.7. STAGES OF INNOVATION

All organisational players (senior managers, middle/project managers, and operational employees) are involved in the change process as innovation progresses through the stages of accumulation and resolution of ideas (assimilation), adoption, adaption, acceptance, routinisation, and infusion.[10]

Sherif and Menon[11] contend that all organisational actors must be involved in order to increase the capacity for assimilating innovation, yet it is essential that the right interventions are made at each stage of the innovation-assimilation process.

A culture shift is necessary for innovation[12] to become commonplace and integrated into daily working procedures. Employees must be willing to change and adopt new behavioural and attitude stances.

In conclusion, strategy, process, and cultural adjustments must go hand in hand with the absorption of innovation. These are made possible by actors at multiple organisational levels, which leads to quicker and more fruitful innovation.

## 3.8. INTER-CULTURAL TEAMS

We have argued that the globalisation of the workforce, due to the variety of viewpoints, is one of the most important sources of creativity. Traditional idiosyncratic paradigms are being tested, and the team is now able to innovate greatly because of ethnic variety.

The conventional thinking holds that teams of executives or managers should have good teamwork skills. A tempting tactic is to get everyone to think the same way, but our research shows that true innovation occurs when cultural differences are integrated to cooperate with one another.

The significance of bringing these opposites together forms the basis of new approaches to innovation. We have discovered that there is too much

---

10 Cooper, R. B., & Zmud, R. W. (1990). Information technology implementation research: A techno-logical diffusion approach. Management Science, 36(2), 123–139. doi:10.1287/mnsc.36.2.123.

11 Sherif and Menon, 2004: Managing technology and administration innovations: Four case studies on software reuse, Journal of the Association of Information Systems, Vol 5, Number 7.

12 Leonard-Barton, D., and Deschamps, I. (1988). "Managerial influence in the implementation of new technology." Management Science, Volume 34, Number 10, October, pp. 1252–1265.

one-dimensional thinking across too many of these frameworks and claimed answers, much like with MBTI, Kirton, and other linear models. It's common practice to categorise persons as either 'universalistic' or 'particularistic' in cultural assessments. However, why can't a 'universalist' also act in a 'particularistic' manner? And if you're 'individualistic', can't you also be 'collectivistic' and collaborate well with others?

Britain and the United States offer good examples. The team role distributions of both populations are similar but the behaviour which British 'resource investigators' enact to undertake this team role is quite different from the behaviour United States 'resource investigators' perform to provide their contribution to their team.

For instance, the British might start with personal contacts they have in relevant organisations or government, while in the United States the starting point could be rights and rules for the freedom of information.

Similarly, some (more western) 'plants' might emphasise the technical merits of their ideas, while easterners might try to exploit their ascribed status (like Head of Department) or academic title to draw attention to what they are suggesting.

Japanese 'implementers' could begin with a 'just-in-time' approach to planning, while Europeans would think in more sequential steps. 'Shapers' in some cultures (such as the French) might display more emotion through body language as they try to explain their viewpoints.

The differences in behaviour do not necessarily indicate differences in team roles, but differences in ways the preferences can be expressed and enacted within those cultures. There are cultural differences in behaviour, but not in team role.

Our concern is that, too often, consultants assume that simply having all team roles present will make an effective team. They ignore the whole issue of how people with different team roles should work together to combine their contributions.

Business standardisation (MBA education, etc.) and a rise in the diversity of cultures in the workplace are both results of business's globalisation. It is incredible how many inventive innovations have been made possible by expanding internationally. Though many international teams resulting from mergers and acquisitions have failed, those that have succeeded have brought great innovative results.

But is fostering global and inter-cultural teams really that easy? If members of a team play different roles and have different cultural orientations, then the team is full of potential conflict and misunderstanding. Globally we have found the Anglo Saxon world of the United States and the United Kingdom tends to be more individualistic, while Asians take to a more communal teamwork approach. So as long as the Americans remain in America managing all-American teams while, for example, the Chinese stay in China doing the same, then conflict and misunderstanding is at least on the local level. But in today's multicultural world, an American leader could be running a team of Thai, Chinese, French, and English members. And furthermore, what if the senior management group already in place come with an imbalance of team roles?

When we begin to incorporate non-western types of logic, such as Yin Yang or Taoism, we soon realise that we have all been restrictive in basing any profiling on bi-modal dimensions. We recognised these limitations in earlier versions of our own cross-cultural frameworks. For example, we were trying to place respondents along a scale with 'individualism' at one end and 'communitarianism' at the other. But in a multicultural environment, a highly individualised leader will agonise over the fact that many subordinates prefer to work with their team. Conversely, the group-oriented leader will fail because of an apparent lack of recognising the efforts of individuals. Thus we have a dilemma between the seemingly opposing orientations of individualism and communitarianism.

We have investigated how well organisations and their teams reconcile these seemingly opposing views by extending our own instruments to explore how well everyone works together in their team to help the organisation, but where teams encourage, stimulate, reward, and celebrate individual contributions. And this is just one of the examples. Teams that are innovative reconcile the tensions that are created by the diversity of cultures from which its members come.

[Readers can explore these generic cultural dimensions and profile themselves with our App 'Culture for Business' on our main website www.thtconsulting.com.

## 3.9. THE SEVEN CULTURAL DIMENSIONS OF INNOVATION

We now discuss our generic seven dimensions of culture, but specifically in the context of innovation.

In approaching a model of competence for teams to become innovative by taking advantage of their diversity, we have applied our seven-dimensional model of culture, which we've described more generically in earlier works. Each has contrasting value poles. These are selected because we have found that they best account for the major differences between national cultures from our research on innovation. The seven dimensions are listed below in Table 4:

Each of these seven dimensions can be polarised with each other, producing spectacular, amusing, and sometimes tragic contrasts; alternatively, all seven can be integrated and synergised, in which case we achieve team innovation.

**Table 4.   Cultural Differences in Innovation.**

| On the One Hand | | On the Other Hand |
|---|---|---|
| 1. Rule making (universalism) | | Exception finding (particularism) |
| 2. Self-interest and personal fulfilment (individualism) | | Group interest and social concern (communitarianism) |
| 3. Emotions Inhibited (neutral) | | Emotions expressed (affective) |
| 4. Preference for precise, singular 'hard' standards (specificity) | versus ... | Preference for pervasive, patterned and 'soft' processes (diffusion) |
| 5. Control and effective direction comes from within (inner-directed) | | Control and effective direction comes from outside (outer-directed) |
| 6. Status earned through success and track record (achievement) | | Status ascribed to person's potential, e.g. age, family, education (ascription) |
| 7. Time is conceived of as a 'race' with passing increments (sequential) | | Time is conceived of as a 'dance' with circular iterations (synchronous) |

The challenge for teams and their leaders to become successfully innovative is to integrate the value differences as we have been discussing.

New approaches to achieving an innovation mind set comes from exploring these tensions and their reconciliations as summarised below:

1. We first contrasted rule making and exception finding but then argued that they are integratable. You use exceptions to improve rules and rules to recognise what is genuinely exceptional. We call this learning revising rules to accommodate exceptions.

2. We then contrasted competitive individualism with the requirement that communities co-operate and argued that these were integratable. It is possible to compete at co-operating with customers and/or within your team. It is possible for communities to develop and to celebrate their outstanding individual members. Competing helps us to differentiate best practices. Co-operating helps us disseminate and adopt the best. We called this learning co-opetition.

3. We contrasted the preferences for analysing issues into specifics and synthesising, elaborating these into diffuse wholes, and argued that these were integratable. You have to allow self-organising knowledge,

values and team processes flow diffusely, then supply detailed, specific feedback on their effectiveness. We call this learning co-evolution with corrective feedback.

4. We contrasted neutral and rational with affective forms of expression, in which feelings are fully owned, and argued that these were integratable. You cannot think about your emotions unless these are owned, expressed and shared, but you also have to control yourself until the right moment and circumstances. We agree with Pascale that the heart has its reason.

5. We contrasted two sources of experienced control: that from inside us, inner-directed, and that from outside us, outer-directed. Strategy, for example, could be designed from within top management, or it could emerge from the company's interface with customers, outside top management. We argued that these processes were integratable. Top management could use its inner resources to design and reshape the strategies emerging outside, which had already pleased customers. We called this crafted strategy, in honour of Henry Mintzberg, as when the clay rises spontaneously from the rotating potter's wheel.

6. We contrasted status earned through achievement with status ascribed to the person's potential, that is, age, family, and argued that these were integratable. The more you respect a person's potential and the more you invest in training them, the more likely they are to reciprocate by achieving on behalf of the company. We called this mentored achievement.

7. Finally, we contrasted a sequential view of time as some kind of race against the clock, with a synchronous view of time, as in a finely choreographed dance. We saw that these were integratable, as when by synchronising processes just-in-time you 'shorten the race-course' by way of parallel processing, before combining these in final assembly. We called this flexible manufacturing or, in a market context, pull strategy.

Not only do these seven integrations constitute a conceptual model of transcultural competence, but they also represent a framework for 'valuing' in general, wherein the preferences and stereotypes of a culture are relative, while the need to integrate values is absolute and essential to civic society as well as to wealth creation. The danger of stereotyped cultural imagery is that it hides this necessity from us. It follows that foreign cultures may arouse what is latent in our own values: they may remind us that what is perhaps overemphasised in their culture is underemphasised in ours. We have the preferences of foreign cultures within our own, albeit in a weaker state.

## 3.10. MEASURING INNOVATION COMPETENCE

We experimented with several diagnostic questionnaires with different formats, but these were all based on the same underlying conceptual framework and research quest: to distinguish between rejecting opposite values, going for compromise, and reconciling by either starting from one's own perspective and accommodating the other or vice versa. We have researched a wide range of organisation types and industry sectors and sought to correlate responses with innovation other business performance variables, such as profitability, costs, growth metrics, etc.

The following trends from the research data were found:

There is a capacity to deal with and reconcile values in general. Respondents who reconcile dilemmas are likely to employ similar logics across the board, as do 'compromisers' and 'polarisers'.

Innovation competence, as measured by our conceptual framework, correlates strongly, consistently and significantly with:

(a)  extent of experience with international assignments;

(b)  rating by superiors on 'suitability for' and 'success in' overseas postings and partnerships; and

(c)  high positive evaluations via 360° feedback. This arguably reconciles equality versus hierarchy, since the verdicts of peers, superiors, and subordinates are compared.

Finally, we can conjecture that transcultural competence may only be the tip of the iceberg, representing the most visible manifestation of human diversity in general. The role of leaders and managers is increasingly to manage diversity per se, whatever its origins in culture, industry, discipline, socio-economic group, or gender. If there is indeed a way of thinking that integrates values as opposed to 'adding value', the implications are far-reaching.

# 4

# INNOVATION AT THE ORGANISATIONAL LEVEL

Of course, it is necessary to have creative people as individuals and teams that are creative, but although these are necessary even together they are insufficient for a culture of innovation.

To foster innovation within an organisation, the key is to establish an integrated organisation culture that can enable, sustain and develop new ideas. This path is challenging and requires overcoming numerous obstacles and crises. In addition, the culture of creativity must continuously incorporate all the essential elements of the organisation to promote sustainable innovation. The dynamics and processes involved in this process differ from those at the individual or team level. However, they share similar dilemmas that need to be resolved, and the methodologies used to diagnose and improve organisation culture must evolve from static snapshots to a dynamic process that manages competing values.

## 4.1. THE IMPORTANCE OF ORGANISATION CULTURE

It has become evident from the literature available on organisation culture that every dominant organisational culture has its own advantages and disadvantages. Our research, spanning three decades, has shown that most organisations like the ones mentioned in our book.[1] 'Riding the Waves of Culture' have a primary organisation culture that faces difficulties in accommodating less dominant orientations. We have identified four organisation culture stereotypes that

---

1  Fons Trompenaars and Charles Hampden-Turner, Riding the waves of culture, Wiley (1997 and later, all editions).

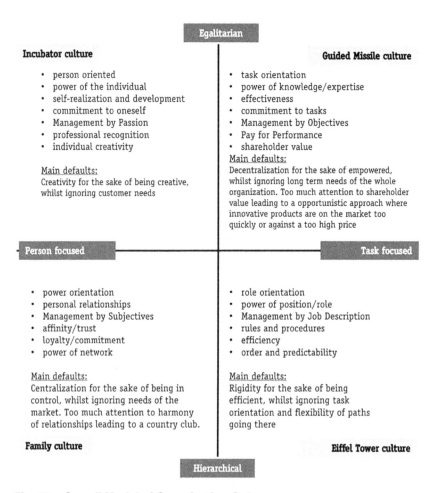

**Fig. 12.   Overall Model of Organisation Culture.**

arise from two dimensions: one being either more egalitarian or hierarchical, and the other being more people-oriented or task-oriented as shown in Fig. 12.

## 4.2. THE NEED FOR A NEW PARADIGM OF ORGANISATION CULTURE

After studying more than 250 organisations of varying sizes, we've found that all four organisational cultures, including Incubator, Family, Guided Missile, and Eiffel Tower, exist to some degree in every organisation. However, one culture is typically dominant. Although sub-cultures may emerge within an organisation, we found no significant correlation between culture and performance or innovation.

This could mean that organisation culture doesn't impact performance or that we overlooked an important variable.

While some scholars, like Jim Collins[2] and Robert Quinn, argue that organisation culture is crucial for high performance, we've discovered that successful cultures of innovation, like those at IBM, Dell, HP, Lego, and Microsoft, cannot be explained by a simple four-quadrant model. This model is not comprehensive enough and lacks the necessary variety. Instead, it reflects a linear way of thinking that appeals to those who understand the world through rational, analytic, and verbal reasoning. These models frame organisation cultures in four general perspectives, such as internal versus external focus, flexibility versus control, task versus person orientation, and egalitarian versus hierarchical orientation. This approach is used in frameworks developed by Handy,[3] Harrison,[4] Cameron,[5] Quinn, and Dennison, among others. They all combine two organisational perspectives in a two-by-two Johari window.

These models tend to thrive because of our bias in how we process information, and because we have a preference for living in certain kind of settings. Because these dominant orientations are so powerful, it is difficult to ignore them without being schismogenic.[6] It can be challenging to acknowledge our own biases and the potential benefits of opposing viewpoints. Additionally, the diagnostic questionnaires used to assess these distinct perspectives often require respondents to choose between them. Many of us are familiar with these types of questionnaires, which typically include traditional questions that offer limited response options.

In this organisation ...

(a)   One is open to the personal needs for learning and growth (Incubator).

(b)   One has a clear division of functions and responsibilities (Eiffel Tower).

---

2   Jim Collins, From good to great, Collins Publishers, 2001 and Robert Quinn, Beyond rational management, Jossey Bass, 1988.

3   Charles Handy, Gods of management, the changing work of organisations (organisations): Arrow Books Ltd; New edition, 2 Feb 1995.

4   Roger Harrison, Corporate ideologies, San Francisco, 1972.

5   Cameron, K. S., & R. Quinn, R. E., Diagnosing and changing organisational culture. Reading: Addison-Wesley, 1999.

6   The term schismogenesis ('creation of schisms') according to Bateson in Mind and Nature, 1979, refers to arguments, theories, or perspectives that are broken or split (schismo) at the outset (genesis). One of two opposing chosen over another.

(c)    One respects the judgment of those in authority (Family).

(d)    One clearly allocates resources and expertise for the job at hand (Guided Missile).

In this organisation …

(a)    Criticism is aimed at the task, not at the person (Guided Missile).

(b)    Criticism is only given when asked for (Eiffel Tower).

(c)    Criticism is mainly negative and usually takes the form of blame (Incubator).

(d)    Criticism is usually avoided because people are afraid of hurting each other (Family).

Regrettably, the conventional social science's empirical basis can impede the development of a more comprehensive and adaptable theoretical foundation that can handle more intricate and practical circumstances. Empiricism relies mainly on a rational-deductive viewpoint that aims to answer the question: 'What is?' It keeps breaking things down to find linear, cause-and-effect connections. As Alfred Schutz[7] put it so eloquently, what is observed is viewed as 'molecules that don't talk back'.

One method to highlight the limitations of stereotypical two-by-two culture frameworks is to push them to the extreme and observe the pathologies that arise. When cultures are confined to one quadrant of the chart, they can become obsessed with the possibilities of their vision over time.

Leaders can place too much value on each of the 'good' criteria and pursue them in a narrow-minded manner. Quinn emphasises that when this happens, a peculiar reversal can occur. Pursuing a single set of criteria zealously can cause good things to become bad things, and criteria of effectiveness can turn into criteria of ineffectiveness.[8] In this situation, the egalitarian-hierarchical and person-task axes, which were initially viewed as neutral categories, take on negative connotations such as anarchy (excessive challenge to authority) versus autocracy (excessive respect for the status quo of leadership) and hedonism

---

7  Discussed in Fons Trompenaars and Charles Hampden-Turner, Riding the waves of culture, Wiley (1997, 2nd edition).

8  Robert Quinn, Beyond rational management, p. 69, Jossey Bass, 1988.

(excessive focus on personal development) versus tunnel vision (blind focus on tasks and short-term results).

It's important to note that these pathologies arise when the tensions reflected in the axes are not reconciled. Ultimately, each of the stereotypical cultures leads to its own pathology, as described in the summary graphic. Effective leaders should always strive to integrate cultural aspects that are not dominant in their own cultural logic. Only then can true innovation be sustained.

## 4.3. TOWARDS AN INTEGRAL ORGANISATION

To become an innovative organisation, it is necessary to reconcile the various organisational cultures and face the dynamic world in which it operates. This approach can help overcome the limitations of the dominant culture, which would otherwise lead to crisis after crisis.

There are examples of 'Guided Incubators' and 'Family Missiles' among the corporations we have studied. Our old way of using a standard questionnaire was no longer effective. Therefore, we created a new type of diagnostic questionnaire that could measure the unique characteristics of each organisation culture and how they align with alternative models.

This new tool explores the interaction between different approaches, using questions that are not just 'forced-choice' but include examples such as that shown in Table 5.

**Table 5.   Avoiding Forced Choice Diagnostics.**

**Please tell us how much you agree with EACH statement**

|  | ++ | + | = | – | – – |  |
|---|---|---|---|---|---|---|
| Each person is given a clear definition of their responsibilities in the organisation |  |  |  |  |  | Eiffel Tower |
| Information is shared widely so that everyone car get the information needed when required |  |  |  |  |  | Family |
| We work in flexible networks in which personal development is key |  |  |  |  |  | Incubator |
| There is an orientation to results and achievement to get the job done |  |  |  |  |  | Guided Missile |

## 4.4. FROM INVENTION TO SUSTAINABLE INNOVATION: ORGANISATIONAL GROWTH CYCLES

Our research and consulting have shown that an organisation becomes innovative when it fosters a dominant Incubator culture that enables the continuous generation of new ideas. When creative individuals are given freedom to explore and experiment, and are led by a passionate entrepreneur, innovation flows naturally. However, our findings also confirm that this type of culture is not sustainable as the organisation grows. To maintain the spirit of long-term innovative capacity, the Incubator must reinvent itself without losing its creative powers.

When dealing with the challenges associated with growth and changes in organisation culture, it is helpful to refer to Larry E. Greiner's[9] well-established model for developing an organisation as it expands. According to Greiner, organisations generally go through five stages of evolution, each culminating in a period of crisis and revolution. To build a sustainable culture of innovation at a meta-level, we must examine these phases and their interactions.

### 4.4.1. Creating Invention: Growth Through Creativity

The initial stage of organisational growth can be described as 'creativity' and is typically led by the organisation's founders. During this stage, the main focus is on developing a product or service and finding a market for it. These founders are often technically or entrepreneurially oriented and tend to view management activities as less important. They dedicate their physical and mental energies to creating and selling their new product. Communication during this stage is frequent and informal, and long working hours are often rewarded with modest salaries and the promise of ownership benefits. Decisions are highly influenced by feedback from the market.

In the past, the big companies that emerged during the 19th century were often led by a vital leader, who was typically the founder. Although the term 'human resources' wasn't used at that time, people did talk about genius, innovation, creativity, and mobilisation of resources on an unprecedented scale. These early manifestations of human enterprise need to be revived in order to replicate their success.

---

9  Larry E. Greiner, 'Evolution and revolution as organisations grow', Harvard Business Review May-June, pp. 55–68, 1998.

As Incubator corporations grow, they face a problem known as the 'span of control'. This occurs when the number of employees exceeds the founder's capacity to know them personally. This can lead to a crisis of legitimacy. To address this issue, rules, procedures, and processes must be established. However, these can never fully replace the founder's actual presence and genius. Although individualistic and creative activities are essential for start-up success, they can become problematic as the company grows. In the past, organisational culture allowed for inventions to become innovations, and resources could easily be allocated to bring them to market. However, functional specialisation separates research and development from manufacturing and marketing, and communication becomes more impersonal. This results in a 'Crisis of Leadership', according to Greiner. Informal communication becomes infeasible as additional functions are implemented. As the organisation grows, management problems arise that cannot be handled through informal communication and dedication. Founders may find themselves burdened with unwanted management responsibilities, and conflicts between leaders can intensify.

## 4.5. FROM INVENTION TO INTENTION: GROWTH THROUGH DIRECTION

As we've observed, Incubator culture that fosters innovative ideas can struggle with scaling up. This can lead to a sense of confusion, and the Incubator can become chaotic and dysfunctional. There's a growing feeling that the entrepreneur/leader and the staff are too focussed on personal growth and developing the next big product or service. As a result, the founder may assume more power and quickly realise that they either find leadership and management tedious or lack the necessary skills to excel at it. This creates a crisis of leadership, prompting the question, 'Who will guide the organisation out of this confusion and solve the management issues it faces?' The solution is to identify and hire a capable manager who has the founders' confidence and can bring the organisation together. This marks the next stage of growth through direction.

At this point, the most critical decision is to find and appoint a competent business manager. Often, this involves bringing in someone the founder/entrepreneur trusts implicitly. In family-owned businesses, it's typically a relative like a brother or nephew, or an interim manager who can address the leadership crisis. However, there's a risk of swinging between two extremes, leading to another crisis of a different kind.

This issue was explored by Kevin Kelly,[10] who did research on how one might best lead a connected network of professional people, each needing autonomy.

The crisis of leadership can be overcome by reconciling the typical leadership style tensions created between Incubator and the Family style leaders.

1. Leading participating employees versus respect for authority.

2. Team spirit versus individual creativity.

3. Effectiveness of teams versus creation of cultural knowledge about these teams.

Let's consider these dilemmas:

### 4.5.1. Dilemma 1: Leading Participating Employees Versus Respect for Authority

In our database of dilemmas, we observe a recurring issue regarding the competing demands between autonomy and direction within the Incubator's staff and Family culture. If employees are given too much decision-making power, it can lead to a loss of democratic leadership with little direction from management. Conversely, if management has too much control, employees may feel constrained and overly dependent on their managers. The solution lies in the form of co-determination and empowerment, which can help reconcile the paradoxes of leadership.

Authoritative, participative, and transformational leadership?

James McGregor Burns distinguished between transactional and transformational leadership. In the former, there is a simple exchange of work for money or votes for representation, with no new creation. In the latter, the leader transforms the consciousness of those led, and those led can transform the leader's awareness. This mutual transformation brings to fruition aspirations that were previously unknown.

The dilemma lies in reconciling the authority of the leader and the degree of participation from employees. Unilateral exercise of power can lead to corruption and shrinking trust from the populace, while too much participation can lead to abdication of leadership. The transactional leader is a compromise, providing routine work for routine pay. However, the transformational leader

---

10 Kevin Kelly, Out of control: The new biology of machines, social systems, and the economic world, Basic Books, 1995.

elevates their followers by allowing them to stand on the shoulders of giants. This type of leadership reconciles the paradoxes of leadership.

### 4.5.2. Dilemma 2: Team Spirit Versus Individual Creativity

The organisation faces a dilemma between the need for creative solutions and individual risk-taking, as seen in Incubator cultures, versus the desire to cultivate loyal teams with a long-term commitment, as seen in Family cultures. This creates a tension between team orientation and individual creativity.

The question arises whether to compete or co-operate. A new term, 'co-opetition', has emerged to describe the merging of these two approaches. Can competing lead to cooperation? Can cooperation lead to better competition? This approach has proven successful in many innovation processes. Teams cooperate with customers and with each other in order to compete with other teams and present the best solutions to senior management for dissemination throughout the company.

### 4.5.3. Dilemma 3: Effectiveness of Teams Versus Creation of Cultural Knowledge About These Teams

Effective creative teams are an important component for fostering a sustainable culture of innovation, but they alone are not sufficient. It is crucial to have a reconciling mindset between team roles in order to succeed. In large organisations, there are plenty of cross-cultural skills that exist within teams, despite often being underappreciated by senior management. While much emphasis is placed on catering to clients' needs, this knowledge tends to remain trapped at the middle-management level and is not shared throughout the company. This practice hinders the ability of teams to learn from each other and accumulate internal knowledge. By keeping cultural information trapped at the team level, senior managers are failing to disseminate valuable knowledge that could be used to drive innovation.

In contrast, knowledge about financial products is disseminated throughout different teams and from HQ to the field. However, knowledge of cultural issues that are specific to each team is not being generalised in ways that would be useful to the wider corporation.

Fortunately, many teams can learn from each other's experiences and avoid repeating mistakes if their experiences are recorded and generalised. Leadership that collects team histories and turns them into knowledge, informs senior management, and develops ongoing cases for in-company seminars and their successors. We propose having a 'historian' in every team whose job is to capture what is learned. This spirals from Action (by a team for a client) to Reflection about that action, so that your transcultural knowledge steadily accumulates at the reconciliation point.

## 4.6. FROM INTENTION TO INVASION: GROWTH THROUGH DELEGATION

The first crisis of leadership in an expanding Incubator is resolved by incorporating individual creativity into teamwork through a new leadership style. This is achieved by conducting talents in improvising jazz bands, resulting in an enriched Family culture where vision reigns and teams work across boundaries. However, the increasing effect of the horizontal axis of person- and task-orientation in the growing Incubating Family leads to the next crisis. Both cultures now lack task orientation which inhibits sustainable innovation.

Although new, directive processes initially direct employees' energy more effectively into growth, it eventually becomes inappropriate for controlling a more diverse and complex organisation. According to Greiner lower-level employees possess more direct knowledge about markets and machinery than the leaders at the top. They feel torn between following orders and taking initiative on their own, and it takes too long for new ideas to be discussed higher up. As a result, employees start fulfilling their own personal and team goals, and the Family culture slips into becoming a comfortable Country Club.

This leads to the second revolution, arising from a 'crisis of autonomy'. Most companies move towards more delegation, but it is difficult for top-level managers to relinquish responsibility to lower-level managers who are not accustomed to making decisions themselves. As a consequence, numerous companies flounder during this period, adhering to ineffective, over-centralised methods, while lower-level employees become disengaged and disenchanted, and leave the organisation.

## 4.7. FROM INTENTION TO INVASION: THE NEED FOR A GUIDED MISSILE CULTURE

The second crisis we face is putting the innovative process at risk, and our leadership is facing new challenges. The Family culture that was once effective in reconciling the chaotic Incubator culture is no longer viable due to our growth and centralised approaches becoming redundant.

As lower-level managers demand more autonomy, we face the next crisis of autonomy. This can be resolved by delegating more, leading to decentralisation. In some cases, the organisation goes public, creating a separation between ownership and management. However, managers struggle to relinquish their authority. This highlights the need to develop a more Guided Missile culture.

To ensure that our innovation process remains sustainable, we must review the challenges that arise during the transition from Family to Guided Missile culture.

They include the following:

1. Servant or leader?

2. How do we centralise lessons reaching us from decentralised locations?

3. Social learning versus technological learning.

### 4.7.1. Dilemma 1: Servant or Leader?

When a company's mission is to be innovative for its customers, the idea of a 'servant leader'[11] is fitting in the business world. When a leader serves their subordinates, they are setting an example for how their employees should treat customers.

If a leader is willing to serve others and not too proud to do so, there's no reason why employees can't follow suit and mirror this behaviour. Servant leaders strive to give away their status and gain it back through gratitude and admiration. By serving others, they lead their fellow servers.

Servant leadership is a powerful way to transition from a Family culture to a Guided Missile culture. Leaders give their followers more than they can repay, creating a sense of obligation and compliance to the leader's wishes. The servant leader is both at the bottom of a deep shaft and at the apex of a truncated pyramid, as they have reversed the organisational hierarchy and serve subordinates as if they were superiors.

There is growing evidence suggesting that servant leadership can contribute to fostering innovation within organisations. Servant leadership is a leadership approach focussed on serving and supporting the needs of employees, facilitating their growth and development, and empowering them to reach their full potential.

Research conducted by Liden,[12] Wayne, Zhao, and Henderson (2008) investigated the relationship between servant leadership and innovation. Their study found that employees who perceived their leaders as exhibiting servant leader-

---

11 Greenleaf, R.K. 1977/2002. The power of servant leadership. Berrett-Koehler Publishers, Inc, San Francisco.

12 Liden, R. C., Wayne, S. J., Zhao, H., & Henderson, D. (2008). Servant leadership: Development of a multidimensional measure and multi-level assessment. The Leadership Quarterly, 19(2), 161–177.

ship behaviours reported higher levels of innovative work behaviours. These behaviours included generating and implementing new ideas, problem-solving, and taking initiative to improve processes and products.

Furthermore, a meta-analysis conducted by Walumbwa,[13] Wang, Wang, Schaubroeck, and Avolio (2010) examined the impact of servant leadership on various organisational outcomes, including innovation. The results indicated a positive relationship between servant leadership and employee creativity and innovation. The researchers found that a servant leadership approach was associated with higher levels of innovative thinking and behaviour among employees.

Servant leadership is believed to create a supportive and empowering environment that encourages risk-taking, learning, and collaboration. By prioritising the needs of employees, providing resources and support, and fostering a culture of trust, servant leaders can enhance employee engagement and intrinsic motivation, which are critical drivers of innovation.

Moreover, studies have also highlighted that servant leaders tend to exhibit behaviours that facilitate knowledge sharing and learning within teams. Research by Ehrhart and Naumann (2004)[14] found that servant leadership positively influenced knowledge sharing among team members. By promoting open communication, active listening, and creating a safe space for employees to share ideas and insights, servant leaders encourage a culture of collaboration and knowledge exchange, which are vital for innovation.

While the evidence suggests a positive association between servant leadership and innovation, it is important to note that innovation outcomes are influenced by multiple factors. The context, organisational support, and other leadership styles can also play a role in fostering innovation. Therefore, it is important to consider a holistic approach when creating a culture that supports innovation.

In conclusion, evidence suggests that servant leadership can contribute to fostering innovation within organisations. By focussing on empowering and serving employees, servant leaders create an environment that encourages risk-taking, collaboration, and knowledge-sharing. However, further research is needed to better understand the specific mechanisms through which servant leadership influences innovation outcomes and to explore its effects in different organisational contexts.

Empowering and inclusive leadership: Leaders who empower their teams, delegate decision-making, and provide autonomy boost innovation. Research

---

13 Walumbwa, F. O., Wang, P., Wang, H., Schaubroeck, J., & Avolio, B. J. (2010). Psychological processes linking authentic leadership to follower behaviours. Leadership Quarterly, 21(5), 901–914.

14 Ehrhart, M. G., & Naumann, S. E. (2004). Organizational citizenship behavior in work groups: A group norms approach. Journal of Applied Psychology, 89, 960-974

by Hu and Liden (2019)[15] suggests that empowering leaders inspires intrinsic motivation, creates a sense of ownership, and stimulates creativity. In addition, fostering inclusive leadership, where all employees feel respected and valued, contributes to a culture that supports diverse thinking and innovation.

The modesty of this leadership style is crucial in balancing intention and invasion. Those with weight don't throw it around and behave as if they are eager to learn from others. High-status individuals exude modesty, which enhances their status, as they have nothing to prove. The concept of servant leaders should not be underestimated in making innovation sustainable for the next evolutionary phase.

### 4.7.2. Dilemma 2: How Do We Centralise Lessons Reaching Us from Decentralised Locations?

The issue of where information comes from and how it should be captured for maximum effectiveness is a persistent problem. When a business needs to communicate its knowledge, it's important to determine where and how that knowledge should travel. Should it come from the bottom up, top-down, from the outside in, or from the inside out? The debate about centralising versus decentralising never seems to end and is rarely resolved. For years, the mantra has been 'decentralise!' However, those with long memories may recall that 'centralise!' was once the rallying cry. Will we ever come to a decision, or is this tug-of-war here to stay? It's clear that centralisation was necessary in the past, but now there is a call for decentralisation that characterises the Guided Missile. We must conclude that both centralisation and decentralisation, taken to their extremes, put the innovation process at risk.

To avoid this contradiction, one solution is to ensure that what is decentralised is different from what is centralised. The slogan 'Think Global–Act Local' provides us with a clue. Decentralise the activities across the organisation, but centralise the knowledge about those activities. The company has a central nervous system, which receives impulses about the diverse local activities. This information becomes knowledge that is stored centrally. If we consider the dilemma step-by-step, we can make progress and extend innovation.

### 4.7.3. Dilemma 3: Social Learning Versus Technological Learning

Is social learning different from technological learning? Can we achieve both?

In Incubator and Family cultures, the focus has been on the human aspect of innovation. The learning Incubator stressed self-development, while the Family

---

15 Online First Publication, April 9, 2020.

was highly person-oriented. However, without a means to depersonalise the process, innovation can become stifled. The Family can turn into a Country Club if more formalisation is not achieved.

Unfortunately, our educational system has long had a divide between the Sciences and the Humanities or Liberal Arts. This same division can be seen in business organisations between those who understand machines (mostly engineers) and those who claim to understand people (HR, Sales, etc.).

This division was measured by Robert Blake[16] and Jane S. Mouton. They tracked the development of managers on two opposing axes: Concern with Task (or technology) and Concern with People. A high concern with Task, taken to its extreme, can lead to a Sweatshop, while exclusive concern with People can lead to a Country Club. However, these two paradigms can be combined, where Concern with Productive People combines technical with social logics. This optimises the socio-technical system, which has been the long-standing mission of the Tavistock Institute of Human Relations in London.

## 4.8. FROM INVASION TO IMPLEMENTATION: GROWTH THROUGH COORDINATION

As a highly diversified field operation progresses, top management may begin to feel like they are losing control. Autonomous field managers may prefer to operate independently without coordinating with the rest of the organisation in terms of plans, money, technology, and personnel. This freedom can create a parochial attitude among lower-level management, leading them to run their own show without coordination.

Eventually, the organisation may face a 'crisis of control' where formal systems are needed to achieve greater coordination. Top-level executives may take responsibility for initiating and administering these new systems. This phase requires a focus on control, which often results in a return to centralisation. However, this can create resentment[17] and hostility among those who were given their freedom.

In contrast, the task-oriented Guided Missile culture has an external focus on the market and is focussed on doing the 'right things'. The Family culture, on the other hand, is focussed on internal political processes of direction.

---

16 57 Blake, R. R. & Mouton, J. S., 1964, The managerial grid, Houston: Gulf Publishing.

17 Larry E. Greiner, 'Evolution and revolution as organisations grow', Harvard Business Review May–June, p. 62, 1998.

The market invasion culture is opportunistic and focussed on doing the 'right things' to satisfy clients, but this can lead to innovative new products being introduced too soon or at too high a price.

During the resulting control crisis, there is a need to reconcile the invasion culture's focus on doing the 'right things' with the role-oriented Eiffel Tower culture. The evolutionary coordination phase involves introducing formal systems to efficiently implement the invasion culture's goals, such as a job evaluation process, focus on product groups, formal planning procedures, initiation of company-wide programmes, investment centres, IT systems, and extensive educational programmes to increase staff's professional knowledge. All these new coordination systems need to become useful for achieving growth through the more efficient allocation of scarce resources.

The invasion of the intended inventions is only implemented efficiently when the following dilemmas are reconciled:

1. The role of standards and benchmarks: should we meet or transcend them?

2. Meeting financial criteria versus developing our people.

3. Focus on external customers versus focus on internal processes.


### 4.8.1. Dilemma 1: The Role of Standards and Benchmark: Should We Meet or Transcend Them?

In most educational settings, the goal is to meet predetermined standards set by those in charge. However, this can be problematic in the process of innovation because strategic objectives are constantly changing. If it takes three years for an employee to achieve the highest standard, but those standards have already changed, then what is the point? The 'Management by Objectives' system often sets standards in stone for a certain period, but this approach can stifle innovation. As Peter Drucker[18] once said, 'Efficiency focuses on doing things right and effectiveness on doing the right things'.

It is important to recognise that standards and benchmarks can become outdated because they are one-dimensional. Once they are achieved, there is little room for growth or improvement. This approach sacrifices one aspect of a problem in favour of another and can hinder innovation.

To successfully innovate, we must ask ourselves two questions: 'Have our people met our standards?' and 'Have our standards met the aspirations of our

---

18 Peter Drucker (2006): The *effective executive*, HarperCollins Inc.

people?' Chris Argyris[19] refers to this as Learning I and Learning II, or 'double-loop learning'. Only when we reconcile both values by creating ever-moving goal-posts can we achieve success. Our people must strive to meet current standards, but those standards must be subject to criticism and updated as necessary to reflect changes in the environment. This is the balance between a Guided Missile culture and an Eiffel Tower culture.

### 4.8.2. Dilemma 2: Meeting Financial Criteria Versus Developing Our People

During our consulting practice, we have provided Management Development programmes for numerous Anglo-Saxon organisations for over a decade. Unfortunately, some of these organisations have cancelled our interventions after experiencing a single bad financial quarter. In contrast, some German companies have asked us to continue our educational programmes despite several poor quarters in a row. To combat the focus on financial performance, Robert Kaplan[20] and David Norton created the Balanced Scorecard, which is highly regarded. The goal is not to balance past financial performance with future learning goals, but to use poor financial results as a learning opportunity, combining people growth with hard financial data.

The Balanced Scorecard suggests that organisations be viewed from four perspectives and that metrics be developed to collect and analyse data for each perspective. Similar to our development of other instruments, we aim to expand Kaplan and Norton's ideas into an Integrated Scorecard. The primary challenge is reconciling the two cultural dilemmas present in the original Scorecard, specifically the past versus the future.

Thus, the dilemma between:

(Financial) and the Future Perspective (Learning and Growth) dilemma

and

the Internal (Business Process) and the External Perspective (Customer)

---

19 Argyris, Chris and David Schön, Organisational Learning, Reading, MA: Addison-Wesley, 1978.
20 Kaplan, R. S., & Norton, D. P., "The balanced scorecard: measures that drive performance," Harvard Business Review, 1992, January.

Following the logic that pervades this lecture, the best support for the vision and strategy of the organisation is found in how past financial performance could not be balanced with future growth but reconciled with it.

### 4.8.3. Dilemma 3: Focus on External Customers Versus Focus on Internal Processes

In order to achieve sustainable innovation, it is important to involve customers in improving internal processes. Co-development programmes, where suppliers strategically align with their clients, are a great example of this. Applied Materials, one of the main suppliers of microchips, has effectively utilised this approach by co-developing systems with AMD and Intel. This differs from the Balanced Scorecard approach, which only focusses on achieving high scores in four perspectives. Instead, it requires a win-win solution that integrates past and future, internal and external values. A company can become paralysed by analysis or cost-cutting, but in order to grow innovatively, it requires a fusion and reconciliation of contrasting values.

## 4.9. FROM IMPLEMENTATION TO INQUIRING: GROWTH THROUGH COLLABORATION

Moving from implementation to inquiry, growth through collaboration can be achieved by entering the coordination phase. This phase involves the use of formal systems, with top management acting as the 'watch dog' for greater coordination. However, if coordination systems become too rigid, a crisis of red tape may occur. To overcome this crisis, organisations must move towards the collaboration phase, which emphasises interpersonal collaboration and greater spontaneity in management action through teams and the confrontation of interpersonal differences. Social control and self-discipline take over from formal control.

The transition of the Eiffel Tower to the renewed Incubator involves the integration of functional specialisations through task forces across functions, as well as giving teams the right sponsorship and span of discretion. Educational systems also focus on behavioural skills for achieving better teamwork. Real-time information systems are integrated into daily decision-making processes, and experiments are allowed to become serious plays rather than just for show.

Progression through this gate will be achieved through the reconciliation of the following dilemmas:

1. Authority of sponsor versus empowered teams.

2. Should we strive to be right first time, or make errors and correct them quickly?

3. Do we learn explicitly or tacitly?

### 4.9.1. Dilemma 1: Authority of Sponsor Versus Empowered Teams

In a culture where the Eiffel Tower dominates, teams are formed when a person in authority sponsors them. However, as companies grow, top managers are increasingly unable to provide all the answers. The world is far too complex for someone who is far removed from field operations to know what steps should be taken next and then issue appropriate orders. This means that team members must increasingly self-organise to tackle a problem that is confronting and disturbing them.

Sponsoring a team presents real dilemmas for the sponsor. They may try to create a Captive Team by seeding it with informers, but such a team, full of people anxious to please the boss, is very likely to be stagnant and unoriginal. What the sponsor fears is the other extreme – a team that takes the mandate it is given and runs with it, tying up the sponsor in knots! Only with care and skill will the sponsor be provided with a creative solution that is genuinely novel. Here, an empowered team presents an innovative solution to its sponsor.

Perhaps the most famous team sponsor was Jack Welch of General Electric. During the peak of team processes at GE, Welch debriefed four to five teams a week and took their conclusions on board. He would implement up to 75% of their suggestions. Sponsorship is no easy task.

### 4.9.2. Dilemma 2: Should We Strive To Be Right the First Time or Make Errors and Correct Them Quickly?

In our dominant Eiffel Tower culture, objectivity thrives. The knowledge that is easiest to objectify is the self-sealing technique or experiment, which can be tested and replicated by others before being sold in the market place. Most people see this as the Knowledge Revolution, a mass of discrete tools that are thoroughly tested and right the first time when installed. This is the kind of knowledge that is idealised by universities and academics in the utopia of Knowledge Management.

However, there is a different kind of learning that is widely used in business and everyday life. Here, we learn through successive approximations. This is the logic that the Incubator is based on. We make errors in our early attempts but quickly correct them. Getting to know customers, learning languages, trying to love or help someone, crossing cultures to engage foreigners, and virtually all entrepreneurship and innovation consist of trial and error.

Trial and error is not limited to inexact ways of inquiry in softer subjects. It becomes important when issues grow complex, and never making mistakes is an impossible demand. This is where model-making and simulations come in. You correct errors in simulations so that you do not have to make them in reality. Knowing that mistakes are inevitable and needing to learn from mistakes, you set up simulations and dry runs. Once you have eliminated errors one by one, you can employ this technique with confidence in real situations.

This process has been called 'serious play'. World-class companies today need play – serious play – if they want to make truly innovative products, argues Michael Schrage[21]: 'When talented innovators innovate, you don't listen to the specs they quote. You look at the models they have created'. The play occurs when inexpensive errors are made in simulated environments. The serious-ness occurs when the perfected techniques are put to use in real situations. As an added precaution, the techniques themselves can be cybernetic and self-correcting, so that 'Houston, we have a problem' can be put right after it occurs. You build into a system the capacity for retrieval.

### 4.9.3. Minimum Viable Product

The 'New Normal' arising from Covid-19 presents extremely challenging dilem-mas for innovation. One is the traditional mindset of the existing organisation or community versus the untested inventive mindset. Another is the related focus on planning and optimisation versus rapid launch and fast learning.

The image below combines and summarises the two dilemmas: is it better to 'aim, aim, aim and forget to shoot', to 'continue to shoot without ever aiming' or to 'shoot aiming', launching an imperfect product, that however fits the needs of the target, than going for continuous improvement as illustrated in Fig. 13.

In today's world, we regularly face the urge to 'go digital'. Client pitches are instructive here. Digital products and services are frequently greeted with initial excitement and followed by blank faces. The fascination with the novel is super-seded by suspicion of the unfamiliar.

---

21 Michael Schrage, Serious play: How the world's best companies simulate to inno-vate, Harvard Business School Press, 1999.

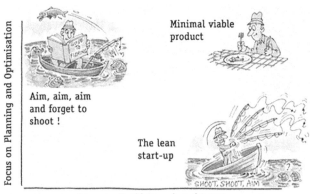

Focus on Planning and Optimisation

Minimal viable product

Aim, aim, aim and forget to shoot !

The lean start-up

SHOOT, SHOOT, AIM

Focus on Rapid Launch and Learn

**Fig. 13.  Planning and Optimisation Versus Rapid Launch.**

By changing wholesale to digital, we risk entering the ultimate niche market – the niche that lacks any customers. In contrast, by following known paths and traditional services, you escape the niche to an open playing field that commands no margin. Neither extreme is attractive: one offers zero revenue; the other offers zero profit.

Possible reconciliations are found in giving the organisation or communities clear traditional boundaries for product development, yet within these boundaries complete freedom can be offered. Experienced mentors set the parameters; young tech nerds experiment within them. The result is innovative products that deliver on traditional demands.

In order to check the degree to which organisations have reconciled this dilemma, we continue to asked cross-cultural respondents to react on the following two statements:

1. In my organisation, we focus on careful planning and optimisation of our launched products and services.

2. In the current crisis, my organisation launches products and services faster than ever so we can learn quickly.

Eric Ries,[22] in his book 'The Lean Start up', introduced the concept of the Minimum Viable Product (MVP) as a fundamental component of the lean start-up methodology. The MVP is a version of a new product that allows a team to collect the maximum amount of validated learning about customers with the least

---

22 Eric Ries, The lean start-up: How constant innovation creates radically successful businesses, Portfolio Penguin, 2011.

effort. Here are some key suggestions and principles related to the MVP in the context of the Lean Start up:

1. Build the Smallest Thing: The MVP should be the smallest, simplest version of your product that allows you to test your hypotheses and gather feedback. It's not about building a complete, fully-featured product from the start.

2. Learn-Measure-Build: Start with a hypothesis about what your customers want and build the MVP to test that hypothesis. Measure how customers respond to it, and then use that data to inform your next steps. This iterative process is at the core of the lean start-up methodology.

3. Validated Learning: The primary goal of the MVP is to learn what works and what doesn't. It's about validating or invalidating assumptions and adjusting your product or business model accordingly.

4. Speed and Efficiency: The MVP approach is all about speed and efficiency. Instead of spending a long time developing a full product, you aim to get something into the hands of customers as quickly as possible to start learning and iterating.

5. Pivot or Persevere: Based on the data and feedback from the MVP, you may need to make critical decisions. If the results suggest that your initial idea is not working, you might need to pivot (change your strategy) or persevere (make incremental improvements).

6. Build-Measure-Learn Feedback Loop: This is a continuous feedback loop where you build a version of the product, measure its performance, and learn from the results. This loop is repeated until you find a product-market fit or decide to pivot.

7. Avoid Waste: The lean start-up methodology emphasises avoiding waste, which includes not building features or products that customers don't want. By starting small with an MVP, you reduce the risk of wasting resources.

8. Continuous Improvement: The process doesn't end with the MVP. It's an ongoing cycle of learning and iterating as you gather more data and insights from real customers.

In summary, Eric Ries suggests that using the Minimum Viable Product is a key strategy for start-ups and entrepreneurs to validate their ideas and build successful, customer-driven businesses in the most efficient and effective way possible. The MVP approach helps you reduce risk, save resources, and adapt your product or business model based on real customer feedback and data 'Make my life Easy' is no longer a top of mind touchpoint. It is replaced by 'Safety', says Mohamed Latib,[23] CEO of CX University. He refers to a hardware store that has been in business for well over one hundred years and immediately recognised this new expectation, this new touchpoint. Say goodbye to speed as a vital 'do it or lose it' business practice. According to him empathy is the most critical soft skill and has been for a century. The current state of our reality has reinforced the enormous awareness of this vital skill.

A letter from the CEO of Planet Fitness addressed gym closures and assisting people with their fitness lives via an app.

Progress in manufacturing is measured by the production of high-quality goods. The unit of progress for Lean Start-ups is 'validated learning' – a rigorous method for demonstrating progress when one is amid the morass of extreme uncertainty. Once entrepreneurs embrace validated learning, the development process can shrink substantially.

Businesses succeed by getting it right in the shortest possible time, using the logic of the integral organisation.

## 4.9.4. Dilemma 3: Do We Learn Explicitly or Tacitly?

In the process of finishing the infinity loop and overcoming the red tape crisis, Greiner observes the need for stronger interpersonal collaboration, where subjective social control and self-discipline take over from the objective measures of formal control through procedures.

Another way of distinguishing 'objective' information from personal knowing is via distinction made famous by two Japanese researchers,[24] Ikujiro Nonaka and Hirotaku Takeuchi. They contrast explicit, codified knowledge with tacit knowledge, shared intuitively between people. The latter is inseparable from the personalities of its creators, although it may later be turned into a codified technique and separated from them.

Organisations promote innovation by blending explicit and tacit knowledge through techniques like storytelling. For instance, the story of Moses leading the Children of Israel across the Red Sea is a powerful narrative with both explicit and implicit meanings that still holds significance for generations. This type of narrative can inspire new insights and meaning, making it an excellent tool for knowledge creation and sharing.

---

23 https://cxuniversity.com/brace-for-covid-19-redefinition-of-cx-touchpoints/
24 Nonaka, I. & Takeuchi, H., 1995, The knowledge-creating company, New York: Oxford University Press.

## 4.10. FROM INQUIRING TO INNOVATION: GROWTH THROUGH EXTERNAL CONNECTIONS

As organisations progress through the stages of invention, intention, invasion, implementation, and inquiring, they can cultivate a culture of sustainable innovation. However, leaders must be aware of the potential for employee burnout due to the intense pressure to innovate. Despite this, a 2006 IBM study revealed a global push for a more expansive approach to innovation, involving a greater mix of innovation types and more external involvement.

Surprisingly, CEOs listed business partners and customers as two of the top three sources of innovative ideas, highlighting the importance of external connections. As technological advances and globalisation create new opportunities and threats, CEOs must prioritise business model innovation alongside product and service innovation and operational/process innovation.

Overall, organisations can foster innovation by combining explicit and tacit knowledge and embracing external connections to drive growth and sustainability.

Christiansen et al. describe the need for 'thinking catalytically', as existing players have resources, processes, partners, and business models designed to support the status quo. This makes it unappealing for them to challenge the prevailing way of doing things. Therefore, the catalytic innovations that will bring new benefits to most people are likely to come from outside the ranks of the established players.[25]

### 4.10.1. Encouraging Collaboration Inside and Out

Regardless of the type of innovation undertaken, collaboration and partnering are very important to innovation. But leaders thriving for innovation have a problem – and it is not a small one.

Despite all the potential challenges encountered when collaborating externally, internal collaboration sometimes proves even more difficult. The inability to collaborate internally can foil companies' attempts to deliver innovative value propositions for their clients.

The financial performance of companies with extensive collaboration capabilities underscores the upside of collaboration. Extensive collaborators outperform the competition in terms of both revenue growth and average operating

---

25 Clayton M. Christensen, Heiner Baumann, Rudy Ruggles, and Thomas M. Sadtle, 'Disruptive Innovation for Social Change, Harvard Business Review, December 2006.

margin. When we analysed operating margin results, for example, over half of the extensive collaborators outperformed their closest competitors.

To outgrow the internal and systemic phase of innovation, when everything is centrally ordinated, to a more modularised and networked phase of innovation, the leader faces the following dilemmas:

1. Internal versus external innovations.

2. Investing in Research and Development efforts versus cooperating with rival companies.

3. Hi-tech versus 'hi-touch' in virtual teams.

4. Systemic versus modular innovation.

### 4.10.2. Dilemma 1: Internal Versus External Innovations

When working with this type of base,[26] the organisation changes from a well-defined entity consisting of fixed structures of managing systems into an entanglement of network systems with fuzzy boundaries. Here the focus shifts from products and companies as units of analysis to people, organisations, and the social process that binds them together in ongoing relationships. Most firms now realise that a key factor in obtaining lasting innovations is not the ability to administer existing knowledge, but the capability to constantly generate new knowledge.

The network perspective is essential in understanding the process of idea generation. The locus of innovation has shifted from individual firms to networks of inter-organisational relationships, where participation in and invitation to knowledge exchange are essential.[27] As a result, organisations are slowly evolving[28] from 'well-structured and manageable systems into interwoven network systems with blurred boundaries'. This trend will presumably continue, making the process of idea creation and the transfer of new knowledge into

---

26 Andreas Seufert, Georg von Krogh, Andrea Bach, 'Towards knowledge networking', Journal of Knowledge Management, September 1999.

27 Walter W. Powell, Kenneth W. Koput, Laurel Smith-Doerr, 'Interorganisational collaboration and the locus of innovation: networks of learning in biotechnology', Administrative Science Quarterly, Vol. 41, No. 1, pp. 116–145, March 1996.

28 Seufert, A., Von Krogh, G. & Bach, A., 'Towards knowledge networking', Journal of Knowledge Management, 3, pp. 180–190, 1999.

network structures, rather than the work of one individual, thus blurring the borders of internal and external innovations.[29]

### 4.10.3. Dilemma 2: Investing in Research and Development Efforts Versus Cooperating with Rival Firms

This dilemma can best be reconciled by a concept called open innovation. We define open innovation as systematically encouraging and exploring a wide range of internal and external sources for innovation opportunities, consciously integrating that exploration with firm capabilities and resources, and broadly exploiting those opportunities through multiple channels.

The open innovation paradigm is often contrasted with the traditional vertical integration or 'proprietary' model, where internal research and development activities lead to products that are developed and distributed by the firm.[30] This challenge involves several dilemmas. Why would firms spend money on research and development efforts if the results of these efforts were available to rival firms?

Earlier models and 'fully integrated innovators' or 'systemic innovators' like AT&T (now Lucent), Bell Labs, and IBM conduct basic research through commercial products. By contrast, open innovation celebrates success stories like Cisco, Intel, and Microsoft, which succeed by leveraging the basic research of others. Under this paradigm, internal innovation is supplemented by systematic scanning for external knowledge, with firms maximising the returns that accrue from both sources. We observe four strategies that firms employ:

1. Pooled R&D or product development;

2. spinouts;

3. product-centric approaches; and

4. attracting donated complements.[31]

---

29 Christian Vintergaard and Kenneth Husted, 'Enhancing selective capacity through Venture bases', CKG Working Paper No. 13, 2003.

30 Chandler, A.D., Scale and Scope, Cambridge, MA: Belknap, 1990.

31 Cohen, W. M. & Levinthal, D. A., 'Absorptive capacity: a new perspective on learning and innovation, Administrative Science Quarterly, 35, 1, pp. 128-152, 1990.

### 4.10.4. Dilemma 3: Hi-tech Versus Hi-touch in Virtual Teams

In the development of an open culture to support the combination of business models and partners, the use of virtual teams has become increasingly important. The use of geographically dispersed virtual organisations, however, comes loaded with dilemmas. In particular, the role of a culture of trust and commitment in the virtual organisation is paramount.

Multiple relationships arising from alliance-based structures require clear commitment to enable the development of trust as a basis for longer-term partnerships. Paradoxically, the perceived low level of commitment from the organisation does not engender the high level of trust and commitment required from virtual teams to maximise their performance.[32]

Charles Handy argues that it is easy to be seduced by the technological possibilities of the virtual organisation, but the managerial and personal implications may cause us to rethink what we mean by an organisation. At its simplest, the managerial dilemma comes down to the question: How do you manage people who you do not see?

The simple answer is, to trust them, but the apparent simplicity of this idea disguises a turnaround in organisational thinking. The rules of trust are both obvious and well established, but they do not sit easily with a managerial tradition that believes efficiency and control are closely linked and you can't have one without a lot of the other.[33]

This is perhaps the area in which balance is most crucial, from both a personal and a organisation point of view. The distant hi-tech extreme can lead to disruption, and the diffuse hi-touch extreme to a lack of perspective; a collision between them results in paralysis. It is the interplay of the two approaches that is the most fruitful for the virtual team: recognising that privacy is necessary, but that complete separation of private life leads to alienation and superficiality; that business is business, but stable and deep relationships mean strong affiliations.

### 4.10.5. Clicks That Stick

Financial service companies are facing a challenge as their services are being unbundled into specific pieces. This creates a dilemma as low-cost specific data

---

32 Liz Lee-Kelley, Alf Crossman, Anne Cannings, 'A social interaction approach to managing the "invisible" of virtual teams', Industrial Management & Data Systems, Volume 104, Number 8, pp. 650–657(8), 2004.

33 Charles Handy, 'Trust and the virtual organisation', Harvard Business Review, May/June 1995.

and transactions are available on the internet, which could bypass brokers. On the other hand, brokers have developed rich, meaningful, and diffuse personal relationships with their clients, creating a high-touch environment that is costly. Merrill Lynch faced a similar situation when Charles Schwab's high-level internet services were eating away at its market share. However, they found a brilliant solution by reconciling new technology with customer service. Their strategy focussed on combining technology with skilled advisors to give clients the convenience of interacting when, how, and where they want.

This approach allowed Merrill Lynch to offer better personal service using high technology to its high-touch customers while identifying high-tech customers for whom it made good business sense to offer high touch.

Interestingly, while high-touch and brick organisations are trying to integrate digital high-tech through clicks, Amazon is going in the opposite direction by opening brick-and-mortar retail stores. Amazon Books, the first-ever physical store, will use data generated from shopping patterns on its website to pick titles that will most appeal to Seattle shoppers. This approach could solve the business problem that has long plagued other bookstores: unsold books that gather dust on shelves and get sent back to publishers. Amazon's deep insight into customer buying habits will enable them to stock their store with titles most likely to move.

### 4.10.6. Dilemma 4: Systemic Versus Modular Innovation

In its years of expansion, Lego, the Danish toy company, wanted to improve its bricks and their possible combinations to help increase sales.

Clotaire Rapaille eloquently showed that Lego found reconciliation in combining boxes for the international markets:

Lego repositioned itself as a source of developing creativity and imagination. If they explained, however, that with one box of Lego, there exist infinite possibilities, consumers would only buy one box, creating a loop. Lego needed to create a spiral, with possibilities for children to create more with two boxes than one, and still more with three than two. Instead of an instruction booklet, they needed a growth map, showing how a child's creativity grows from one box to the next.[34] This is a wonderful example, where the unique guidelines and infinite possibilities are combined with a universal and standardised brick. The international success of this creative tool is unprecedented, and has been

---

34 Clotaire Rapaille G., 7 secrets of marketing in a multi-cultural world, p. 204, USA: Executive Excellence Publishing, 2001.

described by top management as the Tool of the Century. It was cynical to see that at the end of that same century, Lego ran into trouble. Their standardised bricks and tools/instruments were combined with templates of standardised solutions: sales went down, and the rest is history. With the introduction of the internet-driven 'Mind-games', Lego has put itself ahead of the game again, by combining universal parts with infinite combinations.

The success story of IKEA is very similar. As the following analysis clearly shows, making the parts relatively modularised and standardised to make them cheap, while putting them together to the customer's technical skills and taste, made these unbeatable products.

Very much in line with the previous set of dilemmas, we can distinguish between innovation activities that are clearly separable/modular or strongly interdependent/systemic in nature. It is common knowledge that organisations involved in autonomous modularised innovations benefit from decentralised approaches in virtual companies. Mainly through the marketplace, they co-ordinate the information needed to integrate an autonomous innovation with existing technologies, which in most cases will be well understood and possibly codified in industry standards. Such codified information is difficult to protect.[35]

Conversely, in the case of systemic innovations, where the reaping of economic benefits depends on related complementary innovations, benefits are said to take place best within a centralised organisation, that is, in integrated companies that have control of the activities that need to be co-ordinated by means of a hierarchy. Achieving control of innovation activities is necessary in order to control coordination and facilitate rapid mutual adjustment.[36]

As value creation becomes increasingly dependent on learning and the development of new knowledge, it is crucial to improve our understanding of the complexity of the reconciliation mindset in relation to the possibilities for engaging in knowledge-producing interactions. This poses new challenges for management, since organisation strategy must take account of how to support the ability to enter into the right kinds of knowledge-creating interactions, and

---

35 Chesbrough, H.W. and Kusunoki, K., 'The modularity trap: Innovation, technology phase shifts and the resulting limits of virtual organisations', pp. 202–230 in Nonaka, I. and Teece, D.J. (eds.), Managing industrial knowledge. London: Sage Publications, 2001.

36 Chesbrough, H.W. and Teece, D.J., 'Organizing for Innovation: When is virtual virtuous?', (HBR Classic), Harvard Business Review, August, pp. 127–134, 2002.

how to maximise the scope for appropriating the benefits in different contexts. This thus calls for openness in two dimensions: openness towards collaboration partners; and openness towards alternative uses of newly developed knowledge, that is, developing new knowledge with a heterogeneous rather than homogenous demand structure in mind.

# 5

# THE CAROUSEL

After the dominant mindsets of *homo apprendis* in the Incubator, *homo socialis* in the Family, *homo economicus* in the Guided Missile and *homo efficientis* in the Eiffel Tower, the time has come for an organisational mindset where actors integrate opposites: the *homo reconciliens*. It is the actor who works in organisations where opposites, dilemmas, and trilemmas are being reconciled on higher levels. Only then is innovation sustainable.

It is not surprising that recently the value of shares is completely dominated by financial and therefore historic numbers. These determine the rate of the share in combination with the expectations of that same share. Now expected and actual numbers alone can hardly be trusted; we need to find more reliable indices. We have always wondered how the value of an organisation where employees, suppliers, clients, and shareholders meet, can be determined by a relatively small group of short-term movers of money.

But what is a better means of determining value?

Much in line with the criteria of good individual leadership and innovation, we need to fundamentally redefine and rebalance the criteria for the quality of the collective organisation. Many traditional methods for determining leadership qualities and their creative powers base their score on a number of criteria, where the extremes of the scales are mutually exclusive. The ISTJ (introvert, sensitive, thinking, and judging) score, for example, is the most popular typology among successful managers based on the Myers Briggs model. With Shell, it was the more analytic and realistic 'manager with helicopter' quality that prevailed.

But all of these qualities exclude their mirror images. It is not that we proclaim that the extrovert, emotional and perceiving manager or an integrating and imaginary leader with a landing gear should get more chances. In order to ascertain the essential qualities of a leader we need to judge how well this person integrates opposites in tension. The innovative leader will use emotions to increase his or her power of thinking, use analysis in order to test the larger whole and use imagination in order to make realistic decisions. The same applies to organisations in which these leaders operate.

In our consulting practice, we've recently analysed and codified over 10,000 such tensions and dilemmas (from our raw database of 65,000 dilemmas) with which organisations wrestle. We've applied clustering and factor analysis type methods to reduce these thousands of outputs to a core set of 10 golden dilemmas of innovation.[1]

In parallel, we've undertaken many experiments in this area with 10 blue chip organisations. We researched how we could map the value of an organisation in an alternative way, by the degree to which these organisations integrated the tensions over and above conventional linear measurement KPI-style indicators. We sought to discover if such new measurements could give us a much better insight than through the standard pure financial and technical analyses.

In this way, the reconciliation of the dilemma between efficiency of the internal organisation and the development of the employees is of prime importance for the innovation power of an organisation. Here *homo efficientis* meets *homo socialis*. On the playing field of tension between financial short-term results and investments of people for the long term, homo economicus meets homo apprendis. The development of technology needs to reconcile itself with the demand of the market in such a way that the market helps decide what technologies to push. On the other hand, the push of technology will need to help determine by what markets one wants to be pulled by. The need for consistency in the creative organisation needs to be fine-tuned with the need for local flexibility and sensitivity. In other words, homo apprendis needs to be integrated with homo efficientis.

Our last example relates to a simultaneous high score on both specialisation in supply and the value added of the organisation by a broad assortment of products.

---

1  Part of our digital toolsets – specifically our 'Innoscan' see www.thtconsulting.com.

# 6

# SOME CONCLUSIONS AND
# FURTHER THOUGHTS

In the competitive and rapidly evolving global business landscape, fostering creativity and innovation within organisational contexts has become paramount. This comprehensive guide introduces a revolutionary conceptual model aimed at integrating and advancing existing theories of creativity and innovation. The model, rooted in empirical data and innovative frameworks, prioritises individuals' creative abilities, emphasising their crucial role in building innovative teams and ultimately, adaptive, and pioneering organisations.

In our new approach based on the conceptual model, we have described embarks on a journey from nurturing individual creativity, advancing to optimising team performance, and culminating in organisational innovation. Unlike traditional linear and binary decision-making models, this approach embraces a nuanced, connection-making perspective. In a world dominated by replicable ideas and dominant players, as exemplified by IBM's shift from cost-cutting to innovation, this model stands as a bastion of sustainable growth.

## 6.1. CONFLICTS BETWEEN EDUCATION AND CREATIVITY

The prevailing conflict between traditional education systems and the nurturing of creativity is highlighted, with criticisms pointing towards the limiting nature of rigid, 'correct-answer' focussed learning. MBA programmes, often accused of stifling creativity, are put under the spotlight, underscoring a glaring need for practical, real-world, and innovative approaches to management and organisational leadership education.

## 6.2. METHODOLOGY AND INDIVIDUAL CREATIVITY

Our 'dilemmaism' approach forms the core of the methodology, integrating opposing perspectives to explore comprehensive solutions. Data from interviews and a global survey emphasise everyone's potential for creativity, challenging the notion of creativity as an innate, limited trait. The guide explores the balanced integration of analytical and intuitive thinking, exemplified by Guy Claxton's 'hare brain' and 'tortoise mind' model. Moreover, a critical re-evaluation of the Myers-Briggs Type Indicator (MBTI) is undertaken, addressing its limitations in assessing creativity and cultural diversity. The proposal of an Integrated Type Indicator (ITI) emerges, aiming to transcend binary classifications and embrace a multi-dimensional, nuanced, and globally applicable approach to understanding personality and creativity.

Similarly, we have been critical of the bipolar model that underlies the Kirton Adaptor-Innovator questionnaire and what NLP has brought to the table.

## 6.3. ORGANISATIONAL INNOVATION

This book delves deep into the intricacies of organisation culture, team dynamics, and organisational performance. It calls for a paradigm shift that embraces complexity, adaptability, and reconciliation of diverse cultural and operational elements. The role of leadership, notably servant leadership, emerges as a cornerstone for navigating these intricate dynamics, fostering an environment where innovation thrives.

## 6.4. DEALING WITH COMPETING DEMANDS

Various organisational dilemmas are highlighted, touching on empowering leadership, information centralisation versus decentralisation, and the balance between social and technological learning. The text proposes reconciliation strategies, underlining the need for adaptability and a balanced approach to leadership and strategy in fostering sustainable innovation amidst a dynamic business environment.

## 6.5. THE RECONCILIATION MINDSET

A new organisational mindset, *'homo reconciliens'*, characterised by the integration of opposing forces and dilemmas, is introduced. This mindset propels organisations beyond traditional valuation methods, focussing on the reconciliation of diverse perspectives and conflicts inherent in innovation. The proposed 'ROR' index (Return on Reconciliation) suggests a novel approach to assessing organisational innovation power, prioritising the harmonisation of various elements over linear, financial-technical analyses.

We hope the reader finds our ideas a compelling narrative emphasising the multifaceted nature of creativity and innovation. It underscores the crucial role of individual creativity, the nuanced understanding of personality, the intricate dance of team dynamics, and the complex interplay of organisational cultures. In essence, it paints a future where the reconciliation of diverse, often conflicting elements forms the bedrock of sustained innovation and organisational success in a complex, ever-evolving global business landscape.

## 6.6. FUTURE DIRECTIONS

As the world marches into an era marked by unprecedented complexity and opportunities, the guide lays the groundwork for organisations and scholars alike. It beckons a deeper exploration into the harmonisation of the multifaceted elements of creativity and innovation, urging a departure from linear perspectives and an embrace of complex, integrative, and holistic approaches. The future of organisational success, as posited in this guide, lies in the intricate balance and reconciliation of the vast, diverse forces that drive creativity and innovation.

The essence of our approach lies in its multi-dimensional approach to creativity and innovation. By emphasising the need for a balanced, nuanced perspective that integrates opposing forces, the guide provides a pathway to unleash human potential in creativity and drive organisational innovation. The recognition of existing flaws in educational and organisational systems and the proposition of integrative frameworks underscore a shift towards a more holistic, dynamic, and adaptive approach to fostering creativity and innovation. The novel concepts and methodologies presented are geared towards empowering individuals, enhancing team dynamics, and fostering a organisation culture where innovation is not just encouraged but is intrinsic to the organisational ecosystem.

In essence, the evolution of creativity and innovation lies in the complex interplay of reconciling opposing elements, fostering an environment where dynamic tensions are navigated constructively. This is foundational for building organisations that are not just innovative but are equipped to adapt and thrive in the ever-evolving business landscape. The micro book serves as a compass for individuals, teams, and organisations aiming to chart a course through the intricate waters of creativity and innovation, offering profound and pragmatic tools, insights, and strategies.

## 6.7. OUR ONGOING RESEARCH

We continue with our quest to understand more and test and extend our ideas. In due course, we will ask the representatives of the four dominant organisational perspectives – management, clients/suppliers, society, and financial analysts – to provide their opinions and score the organisation on the 10 golden dilemmas according to the methodology and format described below. This is a type of 360° evaluation at the organisation level, akin to 360° competence profiling of individual employees by their peer group. On each of the 10 scorecards, we will ask the relevant group to indicate the relative importance of dilemma for the future sustainability of the organisation's innovation on a Likert scale, so that we can weigh the relevance differently for different organisation sectors or categories.

Our goal is to arrive at a new, alternative 'ROR' (return on reconciliation) index that will eventually push away financial-technical analyses and reconcile the various perspectives. Historical indices will be enriched by future potential. Return on Investment (ROI) will finally be replaced by the much more penetrating ROR.

Let's be just a little creative in the approach and assessment of the creativity and innovative powers of our organisations.

And remember, you can't use up creativity, the more you use, the more you have. Good advice from Maya Angelou[1] who explains why the Caged Bird Sings.

---

1  Maya Angelou. (1984). Why the Caged Bird Sings, Virago; 1st edition.

# APPENDIX

# TEST YOURSELF (OR YOUR ORGANISATION) WITH OUR ONLINE APP

You will have read that the authors are providing free access to a series of online WebApps that enables readers to explore the specific concepts in individual micro-books for themselves.

These are hosted on one of Trompenaars Hampden-Turner's (THT) Culture Factory's online web servers.

These WebApps will typically be shorter versions of the full online diagnosis online (commercial) toolsets from THT Consulting. The aim will be to help the reader (after you have read the volume) explore the content contained in the text of this micro-book you have read to identify how the content relates to your own interest or situation.

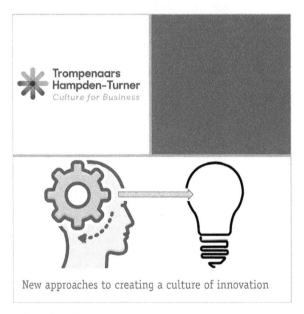

**Fig. 14. App Landing Page.**

You will need a copy of the book to access the companion App to the specific volume. Surf to the landing page for www.thenewbusinessculture.com, (see Fig. 14) where you will be asked to locate a random word in the book, for example, the second word in Section 2 – and use this as your password. Each time the web portal is accessed, you will be asked for a different word and thus require a copy of the relevant book to hand.

Most of the WebApps are fully responsive and thus you can use a desktop or laptop PC, MAC, Android, or IOS tablet or Smartphone.

For this particular volume, both leaders/managers and employees/students will be able to explore their orientation towards creativity/invention and adaptation.

Note we strongly recommend you only access the App, after you have completed reading the full volume in order to derive the maximum benefit.

# INDEX

Printed in the USA
CPSIA information can be obtained
at www.ICGtesting.com
JSHW010731201124
73957JS00004B/9